Max Frisch

PLAYS BY MAX FRISCH
(Published by Hill and Wang)

Max Frisch

THREE PLAYS

Translated by
JAMES L. ROSENBERG

A MERMAID DRAMABOOK
HILL AND WANG • NEW YORK
A division of Farrar, Straus and Giroux

FIRST EDITION SEPTEMBER 1967
SECOND PRINTING FEBRUARY 1969

456789

All inquiries concerning the rights for professional or amateur stock
production should be directed to Joan Daves, 515 Madison Ave.,
New York, N. Y. 10022.

Manufactured in the United States of America
by The Colonial Press Inc., Clinton, Massachusetts

CONTENTS

CONTENTS

DON JUAN, OR THE LOVE OF GEOMETRY

(Don Juan, oder Die Liebe zur Geometrie)

A comedy in five acts

First performed May 5, 1953, at the Schauspielhaus, Zurich, and the Schillertheater, West Berlin.

CHARACTERS

Don Juan
Tenorio, *his father*
Miranda
Don Gonzalo, *Commander of Seville*
Donna Elvira, *his wife*
Donna Anna, *their child*
Father Diego
Don Roderigo, *the friend of Don Juan*
Donna Inez, *his bride*
Celestina, *the madam*
Don Balthazar Lopez, *a married man*
Leporello, *servant of Don Juan*
Ladies and Widows of Seville
Musicians
Servants
Three Cousins of Donna Anna

Place: A theatrical Seville
Time: A costume period

DON JUAN

ACT ONE

Before the castle.

A young man steals softly up the broad steps and peers from the dark terrace into the illuminated castle. From within, festive music. The young man hears someone coming and darts behind a slender column.

DONNA ELVIRA. Hello?

DONNA INEZ. You're completely mistaken, Donna Elvira. What would a man be doing out here in the dark?

DONNA ELVIRA. Hello . . .

DONNA INEZ. I'm freezing. And every time I hear one of those peacocks scream—brr!—it goes through me like a knife.

DONNA ELVIRA. Extraordinary.

DONNA INEZ. Listen. The palms in the wind. Like the clanging of a knife on stone steps. I know that sound. Donna Elvira, I hear it every night, and every time, when I go to the window, every time it is simply the palms in the wind.

DONNA ELVIRA. His horse is in the stable. He is here! I am sure of it. . . .

They go on, and the young man steps forward, but he has to dart immediately behind a second pillar; a masked pair —man and woman—now appear.

SHE. I know you are he!

HE. Who?

SHE. Darling! I'll wager my life you are he. Let me see your hands!

HE. There must be some mistake. . . .

3

SHE. No one has hands like yours.

HE. Ssh! Someone's coming.

From the opposite side, an elderly man and a plump priest appear, and the young man, who had started to follow the masked pair as they left, has to hide behind a third column, downstage, in full view of the audience.

TENORIO. Patience?!! It's easy for you to talk, Father Diego, but how am I going to explain things if the good-for-nothing doesn't show up at all? It's almost midnight. Patience? Don't try to protect my son; I tell you, he has no heart, the same as his mother, cold as ice. Twenty years old, mind you, and what does he say? "I'm not interested in women." And do you know the worst part of it? He's not lying! You said it yourself—his name has never been heard in the confessional. Oh, what heartaches that boy has caused me! "I am in love"— he says this to my very face! —"I am in love with geometry." And this is my *son*, my only son, my heir! Twenty years old, and he has never been with a woman—can you conceive of it, Father Diego?

FATHER DIEGO. Be patient.

TENORIO. You know Celestina . . .

FATHER DIEGO. Sssh!

TENORIO. The most famous madam in all Spain . . .

FATHER DIEGO. Sssh!

TENORIO. Every bishop in the kingdom goes to her place— but not my son! And haven't I paid for *that!* And then when he *does* go to the bordello, what does he do? He plays *chess!* He's not interested in women.

FATHER DIEGO. Easy, Tenorio.

TENORIO. Not interested in women! When I think of it—a Tenorio who is—not a man! Don Juan, a—a—a—a——

FATHER DIEGO. Sit down!

TENORIO. That boy will be the death of me, Father Diego— you'll see—a heart attack.

DON GONZALO *appears.*

TENORIO. Is he here?

DON GONZALO. No.

TENORIO. You mustn't think badly of my son, Don Gonzalo! My son is obedience personified. Believe me, he'll make an excellent son-in-law. It is not my fashion, God knows, to praise my son, but I can not believe—even of him—that he has simply forgotten the date of his wedding!

DON GONZALO. No matter. He has had a long ride and a hard campaign behind him. Yes, I can only repeat, Don Tenorio, what all Seville now knows: Your son has fought magnificently. Without him, our crusade would never have been victorious. I'm not flattering him just because you happen to be his father; I am simply reporting what the history books will say: He was the Hero of Cordoba.

TENORIO. What?! I can't believe it!——

DON GONZALO. I must confess that I myself found it hard to believe at first. You see, my spies brought me the most extraordinary reports of the young man. It seems he was simply making fun of the whole war.

TENORIO. He makes fun of me, too, Don Gonzalo.

DON GONZALO. I called him to my tent. Why, I asked him, just between the two of us, did he think we were conducting this crusade? And when he merely smiled, I asked him: Why do we hate the heathen?

TENORIO. And what did he answer?

DON GONZALO. That he didn't hate the heathen.

TENORIO. Oh, my son, my son!

DON GONZALO. Quite the contrary, he said, we can learn a great deal from the heathen. And through it all this little smile playing about the corners of his mouth! The next time I came across him, he was lying under a cork tree reading a book!

TENORIO. My son, my son!

DON GONZALO. An Arabian book.

TENORIO. Geometry—I know. I wish every geometry book were in hell!

DON GONZALO. I asked him why he was reading it.

TENORIO. What did he say?

DON GONZALO. He merely smiled! Well, I won't deny I was furious. I gave him a horrible order; I commanded him to go to Cordoba and measure the length of the enemy's fortifications. I swear by my honor, I didn't think he would dare to. Absolutely alone in the midst of all those barbarian hordes! I just wanted to see that little smile fade from his lips—just once! *Then* maybe he'd learn to take

me seriously! So—the next morning, as I said, he came
into my tent, unwounded, unmarked from head to toe, a
little tablet in his hand—I could scarcely believe my eyes;
on the tablet was written the length of the enemy's fortifications—940 feet—in black and white!

TENORIO. How did he do it?

DON GONZALO. "Don Juan Tenorio!" I said, and embraced
him before all the officers. "I have misjudged you, but
from this moment on I call you my son, the bridegroom
of my daughter Anna; Knight of the Spanish Cross; Hero
of Cordoba!"

TENORIO. How did he do it?

DON GONZALO. I asked him that, too.

TENORIO. And . . . . ?

DON GONZALO. He merely smiled.

DONNA ELVIRA *appears, masks in her hand, and comes down
the steps.*

DONNA ELVIRA. Gentlemen, the masquerade has begun!
They're already dancing inside—— [*She dances a few
steps, singing.*]

>   I am the girl,
>   And the moon's on the lake tonight;
>   You are the man,
>   As you sing in the white moonlight;
>   Night makes us one
>   And when night is done
>   Love will strike us both blind.
>   With the moon on the lake in the night.

[*She laughs.*] I am the mother of the bride, I know, but I
feel more like a bride than my daughter does. We're the
last ones without masks; take one, Don Tenorio.

TENORIO. Is my son here yet?

DONNA ELVIRA. His horse is in the stable.

TENORIO. Ah—thank God!

DONNA ELVIRA. I saw him from a distance as he galloped up
—oh, your son is the most graceful rider who ever leaped
from a horse's back—hopp-la!—and landed light as a
feather, as though he had wings!

DON GONZALO. Where is Donna Anna?

DONNA ELVIRA. You, too, my husband, must don a mask.
Orders are orders! Don't always be standing on your dig-

nity. Now please, gentlemen, from now on—no more names—otherwise, there's no fun in the masquerade!

The young couple in masks appear again. They embrace. SHE *kisses him.*

SHE. Liar!

HE. By my honor—there must be some mistake——

SHE. Do you think I don't know your kiss?

HE. Who am I, then?

SHE. I'll tell you as soon as we're alone.

DON GONZALO *and* TENORIO, *both masked, have already gone in.* DONNA ELVIRA *draws* FATHER DIEGO *to one side, right beside the pillar behind which the young man is concealed.*

DONNA ELVIRA. A word, Father Diego!

FATHER DIEGO. Who is that shameless pair? I know her voice. I'll swear, it's Miranda!

DONNA ELVIRA. Listen to me, Father Diego!

FATHER DIEGO. Miranda, that hussy, here in the castle!

DONNA ELVIRA. You must speak to her—to Donna Anna, I mean! The poor child is practically out of her mind; she wants to hide herself; she's trembling in every limb, ever since she's heard that the bridegroom has arrived——

FATHER DIEGO. "The most graceful rider who ever leaped from a horse's back—hopp-la!—and landed light as a feather, as though he had wings"?

DONNA ELVIRA. Diego!

FATHER DIEGO. Go on.

DONNA ELVIRA. Well, I couldn't very well say: with the exception of my dear Diego. Quite apart from the fact that he *is*, all joking aside, more graceful than you. In my lifetime—perhaps I've been blind—I have never seen such grace, such youth, such——

FATHER DIEGO. Yes. Go on.

DONNA ELVIRA. Why are you glaring at me like that?

FATHER DIEGO. If our church were not so fussy about the idea of charity, so that it takes away about a tenth of all the alms we get, we priests could also afford to spring off a gallant steed instead of crawling down off an old mule.

DONNA ELVIRA. Diego!—it's not the steed.

FATHER DIEGO. Go on.

DONNA ELVIRA. Oh, you are absolutely maddening! Since
you have become fat and soft, you have also become ri-
diculously touchy. First you were jealous of my old husband; now you are all upset because you're no longer a
youngster. What right do you have to feel like that? I
have never sworn to maintain my unfaithfulness when you
have grown a triple chin, and above all you seem to forget completely that I am married! Married! And if I
should ever—which Heaven forbid—fall in love with a
callow youth, pray remember that I will be betraying my
husband only—not you!

FATHER DIEGO. Elvira——

DONNA ELVIRA. Let's get that clear, my dear friend, once
and for all! Now. Let's go find Donna Anna. [As FATHER
DIEGO *glares at the masked couple again.*] Father Diego,
you are wanted within!

FATHER DIEGO *and* DONNA ELVIRA *go in. The unknown
couple remains on stage.*

SHE. A mistake! How can you talk like that? If so, then
everything between man and woman is a lie, and we are fit
for nothing but to go on all fours, like beasts unable to
reason. A mistake! You think you can fool the woman
who loves you, by donning a mask—you think I will not
find you, the one whom I search for above all others? I
have found you! Must I take off my mask to make you
admit that you know me? If I do, they will throw me
out—— [SHE *removes her mask.*]

HE. Miranda?!

SHE. The whore—yes: for you!

HE. How did you dare——?

SHE. I love you. It sounds so silly: I love you. But it's only
silly that we must say it, because it needs no words. I
have dared, yes, to recognize you out of all of them here,
and now that I have found you, what are you afraid of?
They have all (they think) embraced me, but it was all
like water through a sieve, until your hands came to hold
me. Why do you let me go? You had no experience with
women, you said, and I laughed, and then you were hurt,
because you misunderstood my laughter—and so then we
turned back to the board and our game of chess.

HE. Chess?

SHE. I learned to know your hands over the chessboard.

HE. I don't know how to play chess.

SHE. I laughed, because you know more than all the men in Seville put together; you *sense* what a woman is—and have I not read your face as you slept? Your brotherly face, your face without a mask, which I will never forget— you with your bashfulness!

HE. On my honor——

SHE. Take off your mask!

HE. I've been in your bordello, yes, but, on my honor as a gentleman, I didn't play *chess* there! I swear it!

SHE. Chess is no disgrace. Oh, you! I loved you even before I saw your gray, mild, shy eyes; you are the first man who ever had the courage to come to the bordello and do exactly what he wanted to.

HE. My name is Don Roderigo.

SHE. Of course!

HE. Why do you laugh?

SHE. You have no idea how different you are. And your hands—so skilled they are at being nothing but honorable.

HE. My hands——

SHE. Look how they're trembling!

HE. And if, despite all this, I *am* Don Roderigo—if I swear it by all that's holy?

SHE. Then I will laugh above all at those things that are holy to a Don Roderigo—and hold your hands, which cannot deceive me! I could recognize them among a hundred hands—let me kiss them, they are the hands that once caressed me—not my body, but my face—hands that taught me to know myself, hands that only one man in the world possesses, and you are he—Don Juan!

HE. Don Juan? [SHE *kisses his hands.*] There is your Don Juan—over there.

He points to the young man who had hidden behind the pillar and who now steps forward; MIRANDA *screams as though stabbed with a knife. At the same moment a bevy of masked and laughing dancers bursts out, hand in hand, sweeping across the terrace in a Polonaise.* MIRANDA *is swept up in the dance, and they disappear.*

DON RODERIGO. Juan, what on earth?——

DON JUAN. Listen——

DON RODERIGO. Why don't you go in? They're expecting you, my friend; everyone's been inquiring about the bridegroom.

DON JUAN. Listen——

DON RODERIGO. What's the matter?

DON JUAN. If you are my friend, Roderigo, I beg you to do me a favor—not worth speaking of; for you it would be a nothing—but for me: everything, my whole life, depends upon it. I feel it, I know it, I see it—as clear as these stars: Here and now, this very night, my future destiny will be decided, irresistibly, forever. I've known it for the past hour, Roderigo, and yet I can do nothing. Nothing! It's laughable; we call it Fate or Destiny, and suddenly it all depends on a stupid horse, the whole course of a man's life. . . . Will you help me, Roderigo?

DON RODERIGO. I don't understand a word of all this.

DON JUAN. Take my horse out of the stable!

DON RODERIGO. Why?

DON JUAN. I've got to get away, Roderigo——

DON RODERIGO. Away?

DON JUAN. Roderigo——

Laughter from the castle; DON JUAN *takes his friend by the shoulder and draws him into the shadows downstage.*

DON JUAN. Roderigo, I'm afraid.

DON RODERIGO. Of what?

DON JUAN. I don't know.

DON RODERIGO. Afraid? You—the Hero of Cordoba?

DON JUAN. Oh, the hell with all that nonsense!

DON RODERIGO. All Seville is ringing with your praises.

DON JUAN. I know, I know—the old fool thinks I rushed off to Cordoba at the risk of my life for the sake of the crusade!

DON RODERIGO. Well—didn't you?

DON JUAN. What do you take me for?

DON RODERIGO. But you measured the enemy fortifications——

DON JUAN. An elementary problem in geometry, Roderigo! But never once, as I worked it out in the sand, did the generals understand it. They talk about miracles when our mortars fire and hit the mark—and then they grow furious when you smile at them. [*Fearfully.*] Roderigo, I don't remember what she looks like!

DON RODERIGO. Who?

DON JUAN. Anna. My bride. I can't remember any longer what she looks like.

DON RODERIGO. Well, you have two eyes in your head, my dear fellow, and——

DON JUAN. I've been so happy all day today. I longed for her. I saw her face, everywhere! Even in the blue emptiness of the sky. I passed a funeral—and thought of her— I don't know why. I picked some figs, without dismounting from my horse, and felt the soft sweetness of her lips. She was the whole world! The tender breeze in my hair, the sun at noon, the refreshing coolness of the shadows, the funeral procession with its black box—I laughed and said to myself: "Go on whistling, Juan!" And yet—I rode slower and slower; the towers of Seville depressed me; finally I dismounted and waited beside a cistern until it was dark. . . . [*He seizes* RODERIGO *suddenly.*] Roderigo, tell me the truth!

DON RODERIGO. Certainly——

DON JUAN. How do you know it when you're in love?

DON RODERIGO. My dear Juan——

DON JUAN. Answer me!

DON RODERIGO. I don't understand you.

DON JUAN. I don't understand myself, Roderigo. Out there, by the cistern, gazing into the mirror of the black water— you're right, Roderigo, it's strange, very strange. I *think* I'm in love. . . .

DON RODERIGO. Well, then?——

DON JUAN. But with whom?

DON RODERIGO. Donna Anna, your bride!

DON JUAN. Suddenly—I can't see her face any more. [*A group of* MASKERS *rushes past noisily.*] Was she one of those?

DON RODERIGO. The bride wears no mask. You are overcome by your joy and excitement, that's all. Let's go in.

DON JUAN. I can't!

DON RODERIGO. Where in the world do you think you're going?

DON JUAN. Away!

DON RODERIGO. To your beloved? To geometry?

DON JUAN. Where I know what I know. Yes! I'm lost here. An hour ago, as I was riding up to the castle, I saw a young woman at a window, and I could have fallen in love with her then and there and loved her every bit as much as I do my Anna.

DON RODERIGO. Maybe it was she?

DON JUAN. *Maybe!??* And on *that* I am to swear like a blind man, who cannot see what he loves, so that anyone can come to him and say, "It is I"?

DON RODERIGO. Hush. Someone's coming.

DON JUAN. You won't betray me, Roderigo! Remember: you haven't seen me!

DON RODERIGO. But where are you going——?

DON JUAN *vaults the balustrade and is gone into the shadowy park.* DON RODERIGO *puts his mask back on.* FATHER DIEGO *and* DONNA ANNA *enter, both without masks.*

FATHER DIEGO. Here we are alone, my child.

DONNA ANNA. No!

FATHER DIEGO. Why not?

DONNA ANNA. A man!

DON RODERIGO *comes up the steps, bows to the bride, and recites ceremoniously:*

DON RODERIGO.

> I am the man,
> And the moon's on the lake tonight;
> You are the girl,
> As you sing in the white moonlight!
> Night makes us one
> And when night is done
> Love will strike us both blind,
> With the moon on the lake in the night.

[*He bows again.*] God bless Donna Anna, our bride!

DON RODERIGO *goes in; the* FATHER *and* DONNA ANNA *sit down.*

DONNA ANNA. Perhaps that was he?

FATHER DIEGO. The bridegroom wears no mask.

DONNA ANNA. I'm so afraid.

FATHER DIEGO. My child—— [*A strange birdlike scream.*] That is the cry of the peacock, my child. Nothing to be afraid of. He's not after you, I'm sure. The poor peacock —for seven weeks he's been calling in his hoarse voice and opening his brilliant fan, trying to get Madame Peacock to listen to him. But she, it seems, is as afraid as you are, and she remains in hiding. [*He takes her hand.*] Why are you trembling?

DONNA ANNA. I love him . . . I *do!*——

FATHER DIEGO. And therefore you want to hide from him, from your bridgegroom, "the most graceful rider who ever leaped from a horse's back—hopp-la!—and landed light as a feather, as though he had wings. . . ."

DONNA ANNA. Ah, Father Diego!

FATHER DIEGO. Ask your mother! What grace, what youth, what strength and slenderness, what a miracle! Your mother swears that there has never been such a man, and even if I am dubious of your mother's impression and must remind her—as her priest—that a slender figure is not everything, but that there are inner values as well, virtues of the soul, which outweigh a threefold double chin —even so, there's no doubt the young man who is about to appear here at any second is a magnificent young fellow, proud as a peacock—— [DONNA ANNA *starts up as if to flee.*] Stop! [*He draws her back down on the bench.*] Where are you going?

DONNA ANNA. I am going to faint.

FATHER DIEGO. Good. Then he will catch you and hold you.

DONNA ANNA. Where is he?

FATHER DIEGO. Inside, in the castle, I imagine. He is looking for his bride among the masqueraders, according to custom. . . . The heathens called this the Wild Night— a riotous and dissolute time, says the chronicler, a night of revelry in which each one embraced someone else, at his will, without knowing, or caring, who his partner was. For all wore the same mask, according to tradition, and danced stark naked, men and women together. It was a fearful thing, debauchery like a nightmare——

DONNA ANNA. Someone's coming!

FATHER DIEGO. Where?

DONNA ANNA. I heard something.

FATHER DIEGO. The wind in the palms.

DONNA ANNA. I'm sorry, Father Diego.

FATHER DIEGO. Debauchery like a nightmare, I say, but all that was long ago. . . . The Christians called it the Night of Recognition, and now it has taken on a thoroughly pious tone. Only a bride and bridegroom dare embrace this night, assuming that they are able to recognize one another among all the maskers through the strength of their love. A charming and a worthy theme, isn't it?

DONNA ANNA. Yes.

FATHER DIEGO. Only it unfortunately doesn't work out if the bride and the bridegroom also wear masks; there are too many deceptions in this world. . . . Why aren't you listening?

DONNA ANNA. Someone's coming!

DONNA ELVIRA comes from the castle.

DONNA ELVIRA. Father Diego! Father Diego! Oh, thank God, there you are!

FATHER DIEGO. What's the matter?

DONNA ELVIRA. Come! But hurry! Come!

FATHER DIEGO rushes in with her, and DONNA ANNA sits suddenly alone on the stone bench in the night. The peacock repeats his fearful cry. DONNA ANNA, suddenly seized with terror, flees silently over the same balustrade as DON JUAN, evidently in hopes of escaping him. And at almost the same moment DONNA ELVIRA comes back.

DONNA ELVIRA. Anna, come in here. [*She sees the empty bench.*] Anna? Hello? Where has she gone now? Anna! Strange . . .

FATHER DIEGO comes back too.

FATHER DIEGO. Of all things! Naturally, she's a hussy. But what does that have to do with me? She's called Miranda, everybody knows her name, a poor creature who certainly has no business being here. But what do you want to call me for? Naturally, she belongs out in the alley, but. . . . [*He sees the empty bench.*] Where is Donna Anna?

DONNA ELVIRA. She must be inside.

They go in. The stage remains empty. Music from the castle. The peacock screams once more.

Then the curtain falls.

INTERMEZZO

CELESTINA, *the bordello keeper, and* MIRANDA *appear in front of the curtain,* CELESTINA *carrying a bundle and a swinging lantern.*

CELESTINA. Shut up, I say! And don't give me any back talk! If you don't know your place as a respectable prostitute— here is your bundle!

MIRANDA. Celestina?

CELESTINA. In love! And to think—such a thing going on under my very nose! In love—with a single man——

MIRANDA. I can't help it!

CELESTINA. Haven't I warned you over and over again: Don't fool around with your soul!? I know what kind of a mess "love" is! Why else do you think I'm running a bordello? I know all about your sobbing. Haven't I been like a mother to you? A creature like you—God in Heaven— pretty and worth good money, and suddenly you're fawn- ing like a lap dog and babbling like a poet. His hands! his nose! his toes! and God knows what else! Oh, I've had my eye on you for quite some time!

MIRANDA. If you only knew him——

CELESTINA. Out!

MIRANDA. Believe me, Celestina——

CELESTINA. Out!

MIRANDA. It's not the man, Celestina, not simply that; it's something different about him—I don't know: something wonderful, which you can't understand!

CELESTINA. What I don't understand—ha!

MIRANDA. I can't express it.

CELESTINA. His personality?

MIRANDA. Yes!

CELESTINA. "Out!" I said—for the last time; I don't permit any trash on my doorstep. No one is different from any- one else. His personality! And you have the nerve to say something like that to my face—me, the most famous madam in Spain: You love a personality!

MIRANDA. Yes—as God is my witness.

CELESTINA. Look, do you think you can make a fool of me in the middle of the night, that you can deceive me the way you would a man—or yourself? May God be your witness, fine, but as sure as my name's Celestina I know what my mission is on this earth. Why do the men come to us? There are girls elsewhere, girls of the same age and the same qualifications, married or unmarried, whatever you want; but here, sweetheart, here for once the men get some respite from false emotions. That's what they pay their silver and gold for. What did Don Octavio, the wise judge, say? "Leave the bordello keepers alone! So long as we have our polite literature breeding its false emotions in the world, so long will a bordello be a necessary part of every self-respecting city." A necessary part!—and that means we are officially sanctioned. But do you think the city fathers would tolerate it if Mama Celestina were not on her toes to see to it that everything is fit and proper in this house? Oh, no—I'm not going to offer for sale any girl who is dreaming of another man. This is a place of business, my girl, not of dreams!

MIRANDA. Celestina—what am I going to do?

CELESTINA. Get married.

MIRANDA. Celestina, don't make fun of me.

CELESTINA. Go on, get married! I'm serious; you deserve nothing better. You could have been the most famous whore in Seville, pampered and sought after. But no! You must fall in love! You want to be a lady. Think of us from time to time, my girl. Remember: A whore can stay honorable; a whore doesn't have to pretend fake emotions; a whore has some dignity, and it doesn't bother her if her man runs off to another, because a whore, my girl, sells only her body, not her soul—and certainly not to a *man*, in any case! [*A knock at the door.*] A customer? At this hour? [*She nudges the bundle with her foot.*] Take the bundle and get out. And don't hang around crying on my doorstep! Don't try to ruin my reputation! [CELESTINA *goes out.*]

MIRANDA. Oh God, what have I done to deserve this?

Celestina is right; no one could hurt me before. And now, oh God, why do you let me crawl like a beast on all fours, now that I'm in love for the first time, in love like a human being . . . ?

CELESTINA *comes back.*

CELESTINA. Don't cry, my lamb.

MIRANDA. I'm going right now.

CELESTINA. Not at all, my sweet, not at all! No, no! Where could you go in this dark night? Don't cry! You're in luck, my girl, you've been asked for!

MIRANDA. Oh God!

CELESTINA. He only wants to talk with you. . . .

MIRANDA. Father Diego?

CELESTINA. He only means well by you, my lamb; we all only mean well by you. My lamb, my little lamb!

ACT TWO

A room in the castle.

DONNA ANNA, *in bridal costume, sits surrounded by* SERVING
MAIDS. DONNA INEZ *is combing her hair.*

DONNA INEZ. There, that's enough. I'll put the veil on; I'm
the bridesmaid. All we need now is the mirror. [*The* MAIDS
bow and go out.] Why is your hair so thick? I can scarcely
comb it. There's grass in it, and bits of twigs. . . . [*No
answer.*] Anna?

DONNA ANNA. Yes?

DONNA INEZ. Wake up, Anna. This is your wedding day.

DONNA ANNA. Yes.

DONNA INEZ. You say "Yes" as though it had nothing to do
with you.

DONNA ANNA. Where is the veil?

DONNA INEZ. I like your hair, Anna, even if it *is* thick. It
shines like copper. Copper, with black tips! [*She takes the
mirror in her hand.*] Anna, I've seen him.

DONNA ANNA. Who?

DONNA INEZ. Through the keyhole. You ask—who? He was
pacing to and fro like a caged tiger. Once he stopped suddenly, drew his sword, and gazed at it. What a man! And
here he will stand, Anna, all in white, in shining silk! And
you will lift your veil, black as the night, and the priest
will ask: Do you recognize each other?

DONNA ANNA. And if we don't?

DONNA INEZ. Anna?

DONNA ANNA. Give me the veil.

DONA INEZ. First look in the mirror.

DONNA ANNA. No!

DONNA INEZ. You have never looked so beautiful, Anna——

DONNA ANNA. "No!" I said. [*She strikes the mirror out of*
DONNA INEZ'*s hand; it falls and shatters.*]

DONNA INEZ. Anna??

18

DONNA ANNA. Never fear, he said, no other man in the world has a right to you, if you love me, and no other woman, he said, could take his love. Hold me, he said, this is a wedding, yours and mine, our wedding.

DONNA INEZ. What are you talking about?

DONNA ANNA. Look at our shadows on the wall, he said. There we are: man and wife!

DONNA INEZ. Is this something you dreamed?

DONNA ANNA. Oh, Inez, it is realer than all the days of my life, realer than you and this veil, realer than all Seville with its balconies and bells. I don't know how it was. Don't be ashamed, he said, otherwise you'll make me feel ashamed, and then we laughed—I don't know why—he carried me off to the little island, I heard the water playing about his legs, the black water, as he carried me——

DONNA INEZ. Your bridegroom?

DONNA ANNA. He and no other will be my bridegroom, Inez, that's all I know. I will recognize him in the night when he waits for me by the lake. If only it were night already! He is more familiar to me than I am to myself—isn't that funny?

DONNA INEZ. They're coming!

DONA ANNA. Give me the veil!

DON GONZALO *and* FATHER DIEGO *come in.*

DON GONZALO. My child, the hour is here. I'm not a man for fancy speeches. Let me simply express a father's feeling at such a moment with this kiss. [*He kisses her on the forehead.*]

FATHER DIEGO. Where is the veil?

DONNA INEZ. Coming!

FATHER DIEGO. Hurry up! Make ready!

DONNA INEZ *leads* DONNA ANNA *out, in order to complete the preparations in the next room.*

FATHER DIEGO. We are alone. [*Looks about cautiously.*] Now—what's it all about? Please be completely frank, Commander. Why shouldn't we be able to understand one another—a married man and a monk? [*They sit down.*]

DON GONZALO. Well, as I said, we had ridden into the city of Cordoba, where I was received by Mohammed Pasha, the prince of the heathens, weeping over his defeat, and surrounded by his courtiers, weeping as well. "All this," he said, "belongs to you, Hero of Christendom, take it and enjoy it!" I was astonished by such luxury and magnificence. Palaces, courtyards full of beautiful pillars, towers topped by cupolas, gardens full of fountains and the aroma of flowers, and Mohammed himself, crying as we passed through every room, which he would be seeing for the last time; then he gave me the key to the great library, which I immediately gave orders to have burned——

FATHER DIEGO. Hm.

DON GONZALO. And here, he said, crying all the while, here is my harem. The girls threw themselves down on their pillows, so that I had no occasion to blush—since all I could see was their brown backs. The room smelled of strange spices and perfumes. "All this," he said, "belongs to you, Hero of Christendom. Take it and enjoy it!"

FATHER DIEGO. How many were there?

DON GONZALO. Girls?

FATHER DIEGO. Approximately.

DON GONZALO. Seven or nine.

FATHER DIEGO. Hm.

DON GONZALO. I don't want to participate in a holy ceremony like this wedding, Father Diego, without first having confessed myself.

FATHER DIEGO. Of course.

DON GONZALO. It's about my marriage.

FATHER DIEGO. You astonish me.

DON GONZALO. For seventeen years I have been a faithful husband——

FATHER DIEGO. That is precisely what the heathens don't want to believe of us. They say we have conquered Cordoba simply to plunder it, and they will not admit that we offer them in return the moral values of our culture, such as our concept of marriage. . . . You really astonish me, Don Gonzalo, you are the symbol of the one perfect marriage that we can show to the heathens; the heathens with their immoral harems naturally find it easy to make jokes about our little scandals here in Seville. But I always say: If our Christian Spain did not have a hero like you, Don

Gonzalo, a man who has demonstrated to us the possibility of marriage, unshakable as stone . . . But go on, go on!

DON GONZALO. All this, he said, belongs to you——

FATHER DIEGO. "Take it and enjoy it!" And you stood alone in the harem, breathing strange perfumes.

DON GONZALO. Yes.

FATHER DIEGO. Continue.

DON GONZALO. The girls understood only Arabic. Otherwise things would not have gone as far as they did.

FATHER DIEGO. How far?

DON GONZALO. While they were undressing me, how could I explain to them that I was married—and what that means in our society?

FATHER DIEGO. The girls undressed you?

DON GONZALO. Mohammed had taught them to do so.

FATHER DIEGO. Go on.

DON GONZALO. I must disillusion you: Father Diego, I have sinned.

FATHER DIEGO. That's why we are here: for you to confess. What kind of a sin?

DON GONZALO. A sin in spirit.

FATHER DIEGO. How do you mean—in spirit?

DON GONZALO. I have cursed the true faith!

FATHER DIEGO. And then?

DON GONZALO. Cursed the seventeen years of my marriage!

FATHER DIEGO. But what did you *do*?

DON GONZALO. Do?

FATHER DIEGO. Do not tremble, Don Gonzalo, speak freely. God knows all.

DON GONZALO. What did I do?

FATHER DIEGO. We are all sinners.

DON GONZALO. I-I did nothing.

FATHER DIEGO. Why not?

Now DONNA ELVIRA, TENORIO, DON RODERIGO, THE THREE COUSINS *of Donna Anna, and several* GIRLS, ALTAR BOYS, *and* TROMBONISTS—*all in resplendent costume—enter.*

DONNA ELVIRA. We are ready, husband mine! With incense and trombones, just as it was seventeen years ago——

DON GONZALO. Where is the bridegroom?

DONNA ELVIRA. We are only young once. Which is laughable, I know. For I feel younger than ever, really, and yet mature enough to be fully conscious of my youth and not childlike, like our bride, trembling because she doesn't know what she wants, childlike and confused, whereas a woman like me. . . .

DON GONZALO. I asked about the bridegroom.

DONNA ELVIRA. He's divinely handsome!

DON RODERIGO steps forward.

DON RODERIGO. Don Juan, my noble friend, asks your forgiveness for having missed last night's celebration. He was weary after his long ride, he said, and wanted to rest briefly before greeting his bride and her honored parents. So it happened that he spent the night asleep in the park —until Father Diego, climbing over the high walls in the gray dawn, got his foot caught in the ivy, coughed, and awakened him.

DONNA ELVIRA. What were you doing there, Father Diego?

DON RODERIGO. It is this, Don Gonzalo, which my noble friend beseeches me to say to you. He dares not appear at his wedding until he has assured himself of your indulgence concerning the slight misunderstanding of the previous night.

DON GONZALO nods. DON RODERIGO withdraws.

DONNA ELVIRA. He is not sure of himself! Just imagine! He is the most bashful boy I have ever seen! Just now I surprised him in the loggia—I came up on him from behind. "Why are you biting your fingernails?" I asked him, and he simply stared at me. "Donna Anna?" he said, as though I could be she, as though he couldn't remember what she looked like. And then he didn't say a word as I snatched up my gown and went—simply stared after me. He's so confused, so wrapped up in himself——

TENORIO. Let's hope so.

DONNA ELVIRA. Like a criminal before a trial.

DON RODERIGO returns with DON JUAN. Trombones accompany the ceremony of greeting.

TENORIO. My son! It is traditional that I should say a few words at this time, although, God knows, my heart is

almost bursting as I see you for the first time clad as a
bridegroom—to begin with, my honored friends already
understand what I want to say: For the first time, and let
us hope for the last time, my son——

DONNA ELVIRA. We understand.

TENORIO. According to tradition——

FATHER DIEGO. Make it short.

TENORIO. God grant! God grant! [*He blesses his son.*]

DON GONZALO. My boy! The hour is here. I too am not a
man of many words or fancy speeches, but what I say
comes from the heart—— [DON GONZALO *falls silent.*]

DONNA ELVIRA. Tell them to blow the trombones, Father
Diego. He won't be able to think of anything more.

The two fathers embrace one another emotionally.

TENORIO. God grant!

DON GONZALO. God grant!

*The trombones blast; all fall to their knees—excepting the
priest and the bridegroom. The bride, led by* DONNA
INEZ, *enters, veiled. The ceremony, which is beautiful, con-
cludes with the bride and the bridegroom facing one another,* FATHER DIEGO *between them.*

FATHER DIEGO. "Oh, Lord, who is worthy to dwell in Thy
tents and walk on Thy holy hills? He who treads blameless
paths, practices justice, and speaks truth from his heart—
who abides by Thy words, even in sorrow and despair—he
who does so, need never fear." Amen [*Trombones.*]
Thou: Donna Anna, daughter of Don Gonzalo de Ulloa,
Commander of Seville—and thou: Don Juan Tenorio,
son of Don Pedro Tenorio, banker—you two, clad as
bride and bridegroom, hither come according to the
free impulse of your hearts in order to speak the truth
before God, your Lord and Creator, answer my question in clear, loud voices—in the name of the Father, the
Son, and the Holy Ghost. [*He makes the sign of the cross
three times.*] Do you recognize and acknowledge one another face to face? [DONNA ANNA *lifts her veil.* DON JUAN
starts back in surprise; the bride's face shines joyfully.]
Answer, Donna Anna, do you recognize him?

DONNA ANNA. Oh, yes!

FATHER DIEGO. Answer, Don Juan, do you recognize her?

DON JUAN. Yes . . . yes, of course . . .

Trombones.

FATHER DIEGO. Then answer the other questions.

DONNA ELVIRA. Look how he's trembling!

FATHER DIEGO. Since you have recognized one another, Donna Anna and Don Juan, now are you ready to join hands in the union of matrimony, which preserves your love so that Satan, the fallen angel, may never transform its heavenly wonder to earthly pain; now are you ready to swear that no other love will live in your hearts so long as you live, save this which today we consecrate through the sacrament of marriage; are you ready to swear in the name of the Father, the Son, and the Holy Ghost? [*He makes the sign of the cross three times.*] I ask you, Donna Anna.

DONNA ANNA. Yes!

FATHER DIEGO. I ask you, Don Juan.

DON JUAN. No.

Trombones.

FATHER DIEGO. Let us pray.

DON JUAN. "No!" I said. "No!" That is—if you really want my answer. I can't marry this girl—I don't know why, but it's impossible. I'm sorry. Everybody get up.

DON GONZALO. What is he saying?

DON JUAN. It won't work.

DON GONZALO. He said "No"??

TENORIO. My son!

FATHER DIEGO. What does this mean?

DON JUAN. I say, "I don't want to get married." I can't swear the oath. We made love last night in the park—naturally I recognize her. . . .

DON GONZALO. You did *what*?

DON JUAN. I'd rather not discuss it.

DON GONZALO. Made *love*?!!

DON JUAN. We ran into each other in the park, yes, in the darkness, and all at once everything seemed so natural. We were both running away from ourselves, but there in the dark, where we didn't know who we were, it was perfectly simple. And beautiful, even. We made a plan;

now I can betray it. Tonight I was going to see her again,
for we loved each other so very much, and we were going
to elope.

DON GONZALO. My daughter?

DON JUAN. If I had not been so weary that I slept till dawn,
and if this good father had not discovered me under the
cedar tree, so that I had to come here with him, I give you
my word, I would have spared you all this trouble. What
would I have done? Your wedding ceremonies are farces,
I would have said, and then in the night, when it was
dark again—but God knows, I wasn't prepared for this!

FATHER DIEGO. For what?

DON JUAN. This: that she would be the same one——

TENORIO. My boy! My boy!

DON JUAN. Papa, I can't swear what I don't believe—just for
the sake of incense and trombones. Not in the name of
Heaven! And I no longer believe that we—this woman
and I—really love one another.

DONNA ANNA. Juan??

DON JUAN. That is no reproach, Anna dear, and least of all
against you. I don't trust myself. Whatever else may be,
something has been shattered. Now I only know that I
am alone—and that I want to be alone. . . . I can say
no more. The best thing would be to let me go now—the
quicker, the better.

DON GONZALO. Seducer! [*He draws his sword.*]

DON JUAN. What do you mean?

DON GONZALO. Over my dead body!

DON JUAN. What?

DON GONZALO. Over my dead body! As surely as my name
is Don Gonzalo—you will leave this house only over my
dead body!

DON JUAN. For me it is only a step, for you it means
death. . . .

DON GONZALO. Fight!

              DON JUAN *stands motionless.*

DON JUAN. Your wife, Donna Elvira, would like to see me
murder you, I'm sure. . . . Please. Give me an easier way
out.

Don Juan *bows to* Donna Elvira *and starts out the other way, but his path is blocked by* The Three Cousins, *who draw their swords.*

Don Juan. If you insist . . . I had thought we were friends. That's why I spoke the truth, as far as I knew it. Why these swords? I have already killed over twenty Moors in the name of this nonsense you call a crusade; do you think I won't fight as readily for my own sake?

Father Diego. What does he say about the crusade?

Don Juan. Unfortunately, the truth, Father Diego.

They have formed a semicircle around him.

Don Gonzalo. Death to the blasphemer!

The Three Cousins. Death!

Don Gonzalo. Death to my daughter's seducer!

The Three Cousins. Death!

Don Juan *draws.*

Don Juan. I am ready.

Donna Elvira *steps between them.*

Donna Elvira. Stop! Four against one—what are you thinking of? We scarcely know why the boy is so upset. And you, Father Diego, why can't you say something?

Don Juan. What is he to say? He understands me best of all; he has never gotten married.

Father Diego. I am married to God——

Don Juan. You call it God; I call it geometry. Every man places his faith in something higher than woman, if he's sensible. God! Oh, I know Him all right, at first hand, the God of our Spanish armies; only He never realized that I alone saw through the whole business and laughed. Gold and silver for the Bank of Spain, fine—but that we were conducting a holy crusade to bring our higher morals to the Moors—for example, our Spanish institution of marriage—I assure you, my lords, I couldn't keep a straight face. We all know what marriage means in our circle.

Tenorio. My son!

Don Juan. Above all, *your* marriage, Papa——

Tenorio. My son!

Don Juan. Am I not right, Father Diego? You know the daily confessional—not to mention your own little experiences——

FATHER DIEGO. What do you mean by that?

DON JUAN. A bold question in this distinguished company, Father Diego. I don't know how much the Commander knows . . .

DON GONZALO. Eh? What?

DON JUAN. It's no concern of mine, the game that's being played here——

TENORIO. My boy! My boy!

DON JUAN. Your heart is breaking, Papa, I know—you've been saying it for ten years—I wouldn't be surprised, Papa, if you didn't die one of these days. [*To* THE THREE COUSINS.] Well, shall we fight or not?

DONNA ELVIRA. Dear, dear Don Juan——

DON JUAN. I advise you, you heroes of the backwoods, put away your swords; I am no defenseless little Jew that you can treacherously stab in the back because you owe him some money. . . . Donna Elvira, I'm sorry. I interrupted you.

DONNA ELVIRA. My beloved Juan——

DON JUAN. It would be best—I say again—to let me go. My patience is wearing thin.

DONNA ELVIRA. But why do you want to leave us?

DON JUAN. Why?

DONNA ELVIRA. Last night you loved Anna——

DON JUAN. Last night!

DONNA ELVIRA. Yesterday—although it seems a year ago— you leaped from your horse—I saw you myself—and suddenly you were too shy to see Anna. You fled into the park in the night; you found a girl in the darkness, never suspecting that she was your own bride, and it was beautiful.

DON JUAN. Very beautiful.

DONNA ELVIRA. You then—in a sense—betrayed your bride and planned to flee with this other girl?

DON JUAN. Yes.

DONNA ELVIRA. Well—why not do it—now?

DON JUAN. Why?

DONNA ELVIRA. I don't understand you, my dear Juan. Don't you see the joy in Anna's face as she sees that you, the bridegroom, and the midnight lover are one and the same? And you——

DON JUAN. I cannot!

DONNA ELVIRA. But why?

DON GONZALO. Why! Why! There's no why about it! Death to the blasphemer, I say, death to my daughter's seducer!

DONNA ELVIRA. My husband——

DON GONZALO. Fight!

DON JUAN. Begin, my lord, if you are so anxious to earn a marble statue as your memorial. It will remain unforgettably in my memory, Hero of Christendom, the picture of you in the harem surrounded by seven Moorish maidens. "Take and enjoy!" But one must do what he can, eh? Begin!

DON GONZALO. What does that mean?

DON JUAN. I am ready.

DON GONZALO. Are you Satan himself?

DON JUAN. I merely report what I saw with my own eyes: so pale and naked, our Commander with his skinny legs, surrounded by the Sultan's buxom maidens—and look there, the Conqueror of Cordoba, the Crusader of the Marriage Bed, he cannot resist temptation—his hands shake, just as they are doing now—but at the same time, he cannot *yield* to temptation! In short, he can do nothing! [DON GONZALO *lets his sword fall.*] Isn't that how it was? [DON JUAN *turns to* DONNA ANNA.] Farewell, Anna!

DONNA ANNA. Farewell, Juan!

DON JUAN. I am deserting you, Anna.

DONNA ANNA. I know.

DON JUAN. Your mother is right: I loved you, Anna. Doubly. And it's strange to think that I have lost both lovers, both in the same instant, both in you. I only feel that I cannot pledge myself to either of you—or to myself.

DONNA ANNA. We'll see each other again, Juan——

DON JUAN. Perhaps. Seville is small, and the world is not too large. Don't be sad. Life is a long leave-taking, moment by moment, but a happy one—if only we learn the secret. Forget my name and my face, but never forget how beautiful it *can* be—even if only once in your life, for a brief moment. Look at your mother! Become like her—learn to love the world as it is, its brown and red earth that blooms and brings forth fruit, the Andalusian earth, whose children we are. Learn to love all things that die . . . ! I am happy, Anna, that you weep no tears and spare me the stale taste of pity. Tears would only mar your face and anger my soul, nothing more.

DONNA ANNA. I have never been so happy, Juan.

Don Juan kisses her hand.

DON JUAN. Farewell.

DONNA ANNA. Farewell . . . [DON JUAN *slips out quietly.*] Don't forget, Juan: by the lake, when the dark has fallen —tonight—in the dark—Juan?—Juan . . . ! [DONNA ANNA *follows him out like a sleepwalker.*]

FATHER DIEGO. Are we going to let this blasphemer escape like that?

DON GONZALO. May Heaven destroy him!

FATHER DIEGO. Heaven? Even a priest can say that. But why does Heaven have her generals? Action!

DON GONZALO. Surround the park! Quickly! Release the dogs from the kennels and surround the park! Hurry! Hurry!

All rush away; DONNA ELVIRA *and* TENORIO *remain.*

TENORIO. My heart will break, Donna Elvira. When I see my son's behavior——

DONNA ELVIRA. I think he's magnificent!

TENORIO. But me—what is to become of me?

DONNA ELVIRA. I assure you, Papa Tenorio, at the moment that is the very least of my concerns.

TENORIO. My own flesh and blood: hunted down by dogs! And I don't believe for a minute that he seduced your daughter, a boy who knows as little about women as my son does! I know him. This whole thing is some kind of trick to enable him to get back to his damned geometry. I know that boy through and through! Heartless like his mother—she died when he was born—oh, if I die one of these days don't be surprised!

The baying of hounds is heard; FATHER DIEGO *returns.*

FATHER DIEGO. You too, Tenorio! Hurry!

They rush out. DONNA ELVIRA *is alone.*

DONNA ELVIRA. What was it he said about the Andalusian earth? "Brown and red, blooming and bearing fruit—I love it, it is like your mother . . ."?

DON JUAN *rushes in from the other side; we hear the baying of hounds.*

DON JUAN. I'll cut down the whole pack of them!

DONNA ELVIRA. You?——

DON JUAN. They've got me cornered like a wild beast!

DONNA ELVIRA. I am a lady, Don Juan. Put up your sword.

DON JUAN. I don't care if you're a hundred ladies, Donna Elvira—I'm not getting married! I will not be forced into anything—above all, not by a pack of dogs!

DONNA ELVIRA. Who said anything about marriage?

DON JUAN. In the name of the Father, the Son, and the Holy Ghost—I can't swear it—after all I know all that is possible—how am I supposed to know who I love?—and she, my bride, whom I saw with my own eyes: the happiest and most blessed . . .

DONNA ELVIRA. My dear Juan!

DON JUAN. What the devil is there to swear to here?

DONNA ELVIRA. How sweet you are.

DON JUAN. I only know: I am in love—— [DONNA ELVIRA *puts her hands on his face.*] Only—I don't know with whom. [*Suddenly they embrace.*]

DONNA ELVIRA. Juan, my Juan!

TENORIO *enters, sees them kissing.*

TENORIO. My son! My son! [*He clutches at his heart.*]

DONNA ELVIRA. Come! Hurry! To my room!

DONNA ELVIRA *and* DON JUAN *rush out through a door. Almost at the same moment the pursuers, swords drawn, rush in.*

DON GONZALO. Where is he? Where is he? [TENORIO *cannot answer.*] Surround the park!

The pursuers rush on. TENORIO *staggers.*

TENORIO. My boy, my boy . . .

He falls to the floor, clutching at his heart. The door opens cautiously. DONNA ELVIRA *sticks her head out and looks about.*

DONNA ELVIRA. We are alone.

The door closes again softly. The empty stage remains, with the dead father, and in the distance the baying of the hounds.

The curtain falls.

INTERMEZZO

MIRANDA, *dressed like Donna Anna in bridal costume and*
CELESTINA.

CELESTINA. One thing at a time, my dear, one thing at a
time! You're right on the dot.

MIRANDA. If anyone should recognize me, Celestina, they'd
have me whipped and put in the pillory. God help me!
Do you really think I look like a bride?

CELESTINA. To a "T"! I tell you, men are the blindest creatures the good Lord ever created. Good silk, cheap cloth
—it all looks alike to them. I've been a seamstress in my
day, and you can take it from me: What a man sees is
always reality—but he always thinks reality is what he
can't see!

MIRANDA. Celestina, I can barely breathe.

CELESTINA. We can fix that. It's too tight across the bosom
—I see. We'll let out the seam under the arm just a little
—but stop trembling, now, or I won't help you. What
have you got on underneath?

MIRANDA. Underneath? Nothing.

CELESTINA. That's always the best.

MIRANDA. Underwear is scarce.

CELESTINA. These fine gentlemen—they're absolutely comi-
cal when it comes to underwear! A flash of lilac-colored
panties, and they are amazed at your taste. It's just
like in love stories, where suddenly some fool says: "My
dear, we come from different worlds!" No underwear is
better; it's unusual, but it never causes any trouble.

MIRANDA. Celestina, do you really think he'll take me for
Donna Anna?

CELESTINA. Stop trembling, sweetheart!

MIRANDA. I hope this is not a mortal sin!

CELESTINA. Now look how you're breathing—and this dress
is already too tight across the bosom! Just what is it you

31

have in mind? Underneath, my dear, we'll simply take a
seam, so that he can see a bit of your calves. The calves
are all-important. But first, let's try on the veil.

MIRANDA. Oh my God.

CELESTINA. Why do you sigh?

MIRANDA. If all this could only be *real*!

CELESTINA. That is seldom the case.

MIRANDA. It will make me so uneasy, Celestina—pretending
to be a lady—when the cripples scuttle out of my way and
apologize because they have no legs. And the beggars no
longer will yell at me: "Hey there, give us a peso, whore,
what do you want all that money for?" No, now they will
take me for a lady and fear my scorn, and they won't dare
to stretch out their dirty hands under my delicate eyes—
oh God—and no one, no one in the whole plaza will
know that beneath it all I'm still just a wench of the
streets!

CELESTINA. They'll suspect it.

MIRANDA. Why?

CELESTINA. Do you think you're the first lady who has ever
tried to live down what she is beneath the veil? You're like
a child to me—you, with your belief in people; I scorn
it! I tell you: If it weren't for the prostitutes, who can
only dream of such things—where would there be any
room for virtue in this world? [*She lifts up the skirt.*] Now
for the seam!

MIRANDA. Not like that!

CELESTINA. You want me to bend my poor old back?

MIRANDA. Celestina——

CELESTINA. Seven stitches will do it. [MIRANDA *revolves
slowly while* CELESTINA *stands and puts the seam in the
skirt.*] Do you think he'll embrace you, eh? Because he
thinks you are Donna Anna, his bride? Oh, I'll smile,
dearie, when I see you thunderstruck; then your little trick
will collapse—that's the only reason I'm helping you. He'll
have an awkward conscience, that's all, when he recognizes his bride; a lot of poor excuses, a flood of lies, and
no time for embraces, nothing in the way of pleasure—
you overrate husbands, my sweet; all you know is how
they are when they come here. [*The seam is finished.*]
There!

MIRANDA. Thanks.

CELESTINA. Now—how does the little bride feel?

MIRANDA. Oh, God . . .

CELESTINA. Sighs suggest innocence and always make you feel better; you're a better person for suffering—— [*A ring.*] Another customer?

MIRANDA. Give me the mirror!

CELESTINA *goes*; MIRANDA *is left alone with the mirror.*

MIRANDA. How lovely you are, Donna Anna! With your lace on, I *am* you. And how haughty you are, Donna Anna! My mouth is as lovely as yours—although I don't know the taste of happiness. How happy you are, Donna Anna! God help me, I want no more: just once, to be as happy as a bride, to be recognized, even if only for appearance's sake. Just once, when he whom I love kneels at my feet and sees these lips, my lips, just once—to hear from his mouth that he recognizes me, that this face is Donna Anna's, that he loves this face . . . my face . . . [*She presses the mirror to her breast.*] Oh God!

ACT THREE

Before the castle (the same as Act One.)

DON JUAN *sits in the gray morning light on the steps of the terrace eating a cold partridge; in the distance, the baying of the hounds is heard. Someone comes in from the park. It is* DON RODERIGO.

DON RODERIGO. Juan! Juan! It's I—Roderigo, your old friend.

DON JUAN. What is wrong, Roderigo, old friend, that you can't even say "Good morning"?

DON RODERIGO. Don't you hear?

DON JUAN. The dogs? I've been listening to them all night, my dear Roderigo, as I went from room to room. They have such persistence; I'm beginning to feel sorry for them.

DON RODERIGO. Juan, listen to me——

DON JUAN. Have you been with your wife?

DON RODERIGO. No.

DON JUAN. That is a mistake, Roderigo, old friend. You should never leave your lady alone. Suddenly an unknown lover leaps lightly into your bedchamber, and what happens? She discovers that you are not the only man in the world.

DON RODERIGO. What do you mean by that?

DON JUAN. Inez is a very sweet girl.

DON RODERIGO. Juan, you're limping!

DON JUAN. Like Satan himself, I know.

DON RODERIGO. Listen to me, Juan—I must warn you . . .

DON JUAN. And I must warn *you*——

DON RODERIGO. Seriously, my friend, something terrible is going to happen if you're not careful, something horrible —something you'll regret for the rest of your life. All of a sudden, it will cease being a joke, and blood will flow.

Irretrievably! I've been skulking about through the park
the whole night, Juan, trembling for your safety——

Don Juan. I'm grateful.

Don Roderigo. At first I couldn't believe my eyes when she
suddenly appeared before me at the edge of the lake—
like a vision of death!

Don Juan. Who?

Don Roderigo. Your bride.

Don Juan. Anna?

Don Roderigo. She's been waiting for you the whole night
Juan. I fear the worst. The girl seems to be out of her
mind; for hours she sits as motionless as a marble statue;
then she starts up and flutters along the water's edge.
"He's out there on the little island," she says, and there's
no use trying to talk to her. And then, scarcely do I turn
my back, but she calls your name. You've got to talk to
her! Before something terrible happens!

Don Juan. I don't know what I am to say to her, Roderigo.
I'm not in the mood for tender feelings right now, and
she knows I have given her up. What else is there to say?
The only thing I feel now is hunger.

Don Roderigo. Hush!

They move into concealment in the foreground. Don Gonzalo *enters.*

Don Gonzalo. Halt! Who's there?

Don Juan. Look! He's so tired he can hardly stand——

Don Roderigo. Sssh!

Don Juan. Tell him to give it up.

Don Gonzalo. Who's there?

Don Juan. He's asking for his death and a statue over his
grave—you'll see—he won't be satisfied with less——

The Three Cousins, *bloody, tattered, exhausted, come in.*

Don Gonzalo. Halt! Who's there?

A Cousin. May Heaven destroy the blasphemer!

Don Gonzalo. You've got him?

A Cousin. We can't go on, Uncle Gonzalo—look, those
damned dogs have chewed us all up!

A Cousin. It was your idea to whip them, idiot!

A Cousin. Idiot? *I* was the one they jumped first!

A Cousin. I haven't killed them, Uncle—not yet.

DON GONZALO. "Killed," you say? "Killed?"

A COUSIN. We have to. It's them or us!

DON GONZALO. My dogs!

A COUSIN. We can do nothing else, Uncle; let Heaven itself suffer by your revenge; we can do no more.

DON GONZALO. My dogs . . .

A COUSIN. We've got to tie them up first.

DON GONZALO. Do that, yes. But now I will not rest till the dogs too are avenged. Tell my wife, when she awakens: I am fighting on!

They go off in different directions, whereupon DON RODE-RIGO *and* DON JUAN (*still gnawing on his partridge*) *re-appear.*

DON JUAN. "May Heaven destroy the blasphemer!" A charm-ing watchword—did you hear? I'm sorry for each dog who is going to be slaughtered in my name.

DON RODERIGO. My friend, let's not mock.

DON JUAN. I mean it. Seriously. They were the best dogs in Seville.

DON RODERIGO. Think about your bride, man!

DON JUAN. Which one?

DON RODERIGO. The one who is wandering over there on the shores of the lake. Juan, you loved her, I know!

DON JUAN. Who denies it? [*Tosses away the bone.*] Mmmm —the best partridge I ever tasted! [*He wipes his fingers.*] I loved her—you're right. In the spring, the first time I ever saw her—here, right here, on this very spot. I sank to my knees, dumb, as if I'd been struck by lightning. I'll never forget it. And then, how she came down those steps, stepping softly, the wind rustling her garments until she stood before me where I knelt. And she too was speech-less. I saw her youthful mouth, under her veil I could see the sparkle of her eyes, and it was morning—like now— like now, Roderigo; and I felt as though the sun were flow-ing through my veins, as though the air were singing; in my throat there was a sort of strangled laugh—more like weeping than laughter; over all: a silence, embracing the whole earth, like the eternity of night. And the earth was like a fruit in my hand that no one had ever tasted, round and tender and fresh. That was love: for the first and the last time. And now, Roderigo, if she came down these

steps, the wind in her garments, and under her veil I saw
two sparkling eyes, do you know what I would feel? Nothing. At the very best, nothing. Memories, ashes. I never
want to see her again. [*He stretches his hand toward*
RODERIGO.] Farewell, Roderigo!

DON RODERIGO. Where are you going?

DON JUAN. To geometry.

DON RODERIGO. Juan, you're not serious.

DON JUAN. It's the only thing that's left for me after this
night. There's no need to stare at me. I've become a man,
that's all, and I am whole and healthy, believe me, from
head to toe. And calm and happy that it is all past like a
spring storm. Now, as I ride out into the morning, the
clean air will smell sweet. What else do I need? And
when I come to a rushing stream, I will bathe in it, laughing at the cold, and then my wedding is over and done
with. I feel free as I have never felt before, Roderigo,
empty and weak and full of a great need for the manly
joys of geometry! [*Handshake.*]

DON RODERIGO. Geometry . . .

DON JUAN. If that word's a little too dry for you (I love
dryness!), call it the art of the earth, or the play of knowledge, measurement, what you will—the calm delight of
science, which is harmonious. Have you ever felt such a
thing? For example, the joy of a circle, the most pure of
geometrical concepts? Oh, my friend, my soul longs for
purity, for serenity! Or a triangle! Inescapable as Fate.
There's no use shaking or squeezing, no point in cheating
—you are given a single figure with three sides, no more.
That, you must work with. Hope, the deceptive impercep-
tible possibility of something else which so often deceives
our hearts, disintegrates like a dream before these three
clear lines. "This way, and no other!" says geometry. I tell
you, Roderigo, I have never experienced anything greater
than this game of proportions, which the sun and the
moon obey. What is more solemn than two lines in the
sand, two parallels? Look at the farthest horizon, and it
has nothing to do with endlessness, really; look at the
blank sea—oh, how broad it is! Or look up at the Milky
Way, and it is space, in which the mind evaporates, but
still it is not infinity, not really. Only *they* can point to-

ward the Infinite: two lines drawn in the sand, which
speak the language of Intellect. . . . Oh, Roderigo, I am
full of love, full of awe—that's why I sound mocking to
you! Over there, beyond the incense, there where the air
is clear and joyous and transparent, the revelations begin!
That is no realm of whims and fancies, Roderigo, but that
which is meaningful today is meaningful tomorrow, and
when I have ceased to breathe, its meaning still shall live
on forever—without me, or you. Only the serene spirit
knows what blessedness is; everything else is but glitter
and deception, believe me, not worth the holding. [*Handshake.*] Farewell!

DON RODERIGO. And the maiden by the lake?

DON JUAN. Some other man will console her.

DON RODERIGO. Do you really believe that?

DON JUAN. Why are you always so anxious to believe only
what you want to? And somehow you seem to think you
can change the truth by adopting a formal manner of
speech or a serious expression—and thereby modify the
absurdity of life with your absurd hopes—Roderigo, old
friend, I laugh at you! I'm sorry. I am your friend, of
course, but why do you assume that I might never itch—
just a little—to test our friendship? I don't want any
friend who is *that* sure of me. How do you know, for example, that I have not just come from Inez?

DON RODERIGO. Oh, stop joking!

DON JUAN. How do you know I'm joking?

DON RODERIGO. I know my Inez.

DON JUAN. So do I.

DON RODERIGO. What do you mean?

DON JUAN. I'm telling you: I was with her last night.

DON RODERIGO. Juan—you're lying——

DON JUAN. No, my friend—I am insatiably curious about
Nature. I wondered: "Am I capable of such a thing?"—
for I know Inez is the apple of your eye. And then I
wondered: "Is *she* capable of such a thing?" And, even
further, I wondered if you'd believe me when I told you.

DON RODERIGO. Juan!

DON JUAN. Do you believe it or don't you?

DON RODERIGO. You—you devil!—— [DON JUAN *kisses him
on the forehead.*]

DON JUAN. Never believe it, Roderigo.

DON RODERIGO. If it were true, Juan, I would kill myself on the spot——

DON JUAN. I know now why I was frightened by my reflection in the waters of the cistern, that mirror of beautiful heavenly blue without a background. Don't become curious like me, Roderigo. When once we take leave of the lie that shines like a glittering surface on the world and no longer see the world as the mirror of our desires, when we want to know *who* we are—ah, Roderigo, that's the beginning of the end, the Fall of Man—and something keeps whispering in your ears that you no longer know where God lives. Don't sink into your soul, Roderigo, or into anyone else's, but stay on the blue surface of the mirror, like the gnats above the water—and may the Lord bless you and keep you, and may His face shine upon you forever! [DON JUAN *embraces him.*] Adieu! It was so nice to have a friend like you, who was terrified for me in the night. From now on, I must be terrified for myself.

DON RODERIGO. Juan, what has happened to you?

DON JUAN. I have fallen out of love with love. [*He tears himself away.*]

DON JUAN *starts to rush away, but at this moment* THE FIGURE OF DONNA ANNA *appears at the top of the steps.*

DON JUAN. What is this?! [*The vision comes slowly down the steps, treading softly, just as* DON JUAN *had described her.*] Donna Anna?—— [THE FIGURE *stops.*] This is all nonsense. I have deserted you. And you stand here on these steps like a memory, Anna—that's all: a memory. I see that youthful mouth, which I have kissed, and behind your veil I catch a glimpse of two sparkling eyes. Why do you stand there as though nothing has happened? I am no longer the one who knelt before you then—and there's no turning back the clock. The fulfillment of that memory, the expectation, is gone—and I know now that love is not what I had expected it to be. Actually, I don't know *what* I had expected it to be. I only know what it is.

THE FIGURE. My darling Juan——

DON JUAN. Go away!

THE FIGURE. Why do you hide your face? You loved me once, Juan, and I still love you. Why didn't *you* go away?

DON JUAN. You shouldn't have come like this, Anna—down these steps. Your look fills me with a hope which no longer exists.

THE FIGURE. My darling Juan——

DON JUAN. Your darling Juan! [*He laughs.*] Do you have any idea where your darling Juan has been this night? With your mother—that's where your darling Juan has been! She could teach you a few things, but even she was deserted by your darling Juan, so full of love, as he sprang from her window to rush to the arms of the next one! With your mother—do you hear? They hunted him down with dogs—as though he were not hounded enough. Then —and I don't even know her name—his third victim on his wedding day: just another young woman, like hundreds of others in the darkness—nameless, faceless—to kill and bury what he had felt before, and then go on. What do you want from him, who can only laugh and forget? And then, since everything was so empty and without charm . . . it wasn't hope that lured him, your beloved Juan, into that last bedroom, not her bright hair and the novelty of her unusual kisses, not even the joy of her maidenly resistance; she defended herself so wildly, so rapturously; the dogs were yelping outside. Oh, the contrast was enchanting, but enchantment doesn't last long, and in her arms it was all so—familiar—horribly so. But at least she had something—the last one in this night of madness—something that no one else has or ever will have again, something in particular that made her fascinating —something extraordinary and irresistible—she was the wife of my best friend.

DON RODERIGO. Juan!

DON JUAN. She never forgot you, Roderigo, not for an instant. On the contrary, we talked about you a lot, my friend, and tasted the full sweetness of our own baseness —until the roosters began to crow. [DON RODERIGO *screams like a knifed animal.*] That is the pure truth.

DON RODERIGO *rushes out.*

DON JUAN. And so, Donna Anna, that's how I have spent this night, while you waited for me by the lake; and now I kneel before you—— [*He kneels.*] For the last time, I know. You have appeared in order to take the last thing remaining to me: my unrepentant laughter. Why did I embrace you and not recognize you? And now you will leave me the image of this moment, the silent image of loss that will never fade—as you stand there in the morning sun— an image that will never leave my heart as I travel across the earth. And so I kneel before you as I did then, yet differently—in my humility, in my guilt.

THE FIGURE. My Juan!

DON JUAN. How can you still believe that I'm in love with you? I thought that expectation could never return. How can I believe it myself?

THE FIGURE. Stand up!

DON JUAN. I don't ask your forgiveness.

THE FIGURE. Stand up!

DON JUAN. Only mercy, not forgiveness, can save me from the world I have made. [THE FIGURE lifts him to his feet.] Anna——?

THE FIGURE. All this—Juan, my Juan!—how do you know it's not all a deception?

DON JUAN. A deception?

THE FIGURE. A delusion of your mind.

DON JUAN. What is?

THE FIGURE. That it is still I whom you love.

DON JUAN. A deception? How can you talk like that? Then everything that has ever been between man and woman is a deception; then we would be worth nothing more than to go on all fours like beasts, incapable of distinctions, unable to remember. A deception? Do you think you can deceive love with a veil, that I will not recognize you, the only one I have ever truly loved? I know you, Anna.

THE FIGURE. Juan . . . ?

DON JUAN. Don't tremble. We lost each other once—now we have found each other again, forever. [They embrace.]

DON JUAN. My wife——

THE FIGURE. My husband——

DON GONZALO rushes in, sword drawn.

DON GONZALO. Ah! There he is!

DON JUAN. Yes, Father.

DON GONZALO. Fight!

DON JUAN. You're too late, Father. We've just remarried.

DON GONZALO. Fight!

DON JUAN. Why?

DON GONZALO. Murderer!

DON JUAN. I understand your feelings, Father; you've been
    tracking me all night, and now it's not easy for you sud-
    denly to reverse yourself, as it were. And you are overtired,
    beyond a doubt; otherwise you would not be so excited.
    Murderer? Certainly it was not I who killed your dogs.

DON GONZALO. Dogs?

DON JUAN. Leave us alone, Father—presently we'll join you
    for breakfast.

DON GONZALO. Dogs, he says—and already he has forgotten
    his own father—before he is even in his grave!

DON JUAN. My father . . . ?

DON GONZALO. Dead from shock—yes——

DON JUAN. You're not serious . . . ?!!

DON GONZALO. And Don Roderigo!

DON JUAN. Roderigo . . . ?

DON GONZALO. Weltering in his own blood, with his last
    breath he cursed you as the seducer of his wife.

DON JUAN. What are you saying?

DON GONZALO. He fell on his own sword. . . . And you,
    whore, not a word in defense of this blasphemer—I'm
    going to kill him on the spot!

DON JUAN. Roderigo—— [DON JUAN, *stunned by the news
    he has just received, finds himself belabored by the
    brandished sword of* DON GONZALO *as though by a buzz-
    ing insect; he draws, angrily.*] Stop! [DON GONZALO *falls
    from a lightning-fast sword thrust before it even comes to
    a duel.* DON JUAN *resheathes his sword.*] His death hor-
    rifies me—I mean Roderigo's. And I had to tell him the
    truth—the truth he never asked for! He never understood
    me, my old friend, yet I held him in my heart—he had a
    soul like bread, plain but wholesome. How often I warned
    him: I don't want any friend who is *that* sure of me!
    Just now—we were standing right here . . . ! Anna, I am
    going to have to flee. The quicker, the better. Seville is
    no place for us now. Who would ever believe that I was
    simply defending myself against him? But Spain is big,
    Anna, and you won't let me go without you!

THE FIGURE. Oh, Juan . . .

DON JUAN. My bride! [*He takes her hands.*] Let us go.

In the background FATHER DIEGO *appears, the drowned* DONNA ANNA *in his arms.*

DON JUAN. Let us go! Just as we swore we would, there by the lake in the night, like children—never dreaming we could go astray. Why do you hesitate? I hold your hands like a life that has been given back to us, more real than before, more full of the terrible knowledge of how easy it is to throw away. Why do you tremble? Oh, I feel this morning's sun and every living thing like a pardoned criminal. Experience has given me a second life! Let us go.

DON JUAN *starts to go, arm in arm with* THE FIGURE, *then stops before* FATHER DIEGO, *carrying the body of the other bride.*

DON JUAN. What does this mean, Father Diego? [*As no one answers, he shouts.*] Answer me! Answer me! [*A long pause. Then, very coldly.*] Who is my bride?

FATHER DIEGO. You ask in vain, Don Juan. She will never answer again, no matter how loudly you cry. Never again. She has drowned herself. This is the end of your wedding day, Don Juan, the harvest of your wantonness.

DON JUAN. God knows (if He exists) : I have knelt, knelt in repentance, and she has raised me up, my bride, whom I have recognized in the certainty of my heart, recognized as the only one I love. . . . This is not true!

FATHER DIEGO. Then take the body.

DON JUAN. She is not my bride. I have married a living creature, not a water-soaked corpse with dangling arms and hair full of green weeds. What's the meaning of this phantom? No, she is not my bride. No.

FATHER DIEGO. Who *is*, then?

DON JUAN. *This* one! This other——

FATHER DIEGO. And why is she running away?

DON JUAN. Running?

DON JUAN *looks around.* THE FIGURE *has started to escape up the steps, but just then* THE THREE COUSINS, *bandaged, appear from inside the castle and bar the way with their swords.*

DON JUAN. Good morning, gentlemen! I welcome your ap-

pearance. My friend is dead; the rabble remains the same
as ever; and I have no doubt that you will erect a monument, a patriotic monument, to this sword-fighting babbler
who sought for it all night long until at last he ran himself onto my sword. And please, don't forget to engrave on
its base his motto: "May Heaven destroy the blasphemer!"
But now put up your swords, so that you may survive this
morning and serve as witnesses at my wedding. Here: two
brides, one living, one dead, and the Father says I am to
marry the corpse, damned through all eternity because I
lost my way in the night, and throughout the future—if
there is such a thing—I must be pursued by hounds.
That's what the Father thinks. But I say: [DON JUAN *steps
toward* THE FIGURE.] She and no other is my bride, she,
the living, who did not curse the wanderer in the night
and then go to her death, but who reappeared for me to
claim—and I have claimed her. And I will go with her
and fulfill my oath. Have I not been blessed by Heaven
with a second chance at life? And if your Heaven now
abuses my oath to force me to marry a corpse—rest assured, I will never swear another oath or believe in one—
never!—if she is not my true bride. [DON JUAN *removes
her veil.*]

FATHER DIEGO. Miranda??!

MIRANDA. My darling Juan——

DON JUAN *puts both hands over his face. And, as* FATHER
DIEGO *lays the dead* DONNA ANNA *at his feet,* MIRANDA
rushes out. Bells begin to sound. At last DON JUAN *looks up
with a strange smile.*

DON JUAN. Don't expect me to cross myself, and don't wait
for me to cry. Bury this poor creature. And don't stand in
my path. I'm afraid no longer. Now we will see which of
us, Heaven or I, will have the last laugh!

DON JUAN *steps over the dead body of* DONNA ANNA *and
walks straight out. As he disappears, we hear his dry, bitter
laugh.*

The curtain falls.

INTERMEZZO

Before the curtain: CELESTINA *and* LOPEZ

CELESTINA. Love is a tragedy!

LOPEZ. My name is Lopez.

CELESTINA. I loved her like my own flesh and blood!

LOPEZ. Don Balthazar Lopez.

CELESTINA. Fled!

LOPEZ. Chancellor of the Exchequer, madam. I can pay any price.

CELESTINA. Fled into the wide world—a helpless soul like Miranda—without my motherly protection!

LOPEZ. Madam——

CELESTINA. What will become of her? [*She dries her eyes with her apron.*] You can't understand that, Don Balthazar Lopez or whatever your name is—you're only a man—but I tell you once and for all, my place is closed—I'm too upset—come back tomorrow.

LOPEZ. Hm.

CELESTINA. Love is a tragedy.

LOPEZ. Hm.

CELESTINA. Leave me now. Tomorrow. [*She goes out, leaving him standing.*]

45

ACT FOUR

A lavishly set banquet table—candles, gleaming silver; in the background, a curtain. DON JUAN (*now a man of thirty-three*) *is present, giving instructions to three crippled* MUSICIANS. *His servant,* LEPORELLO, *is placing decanters on the table.*

DON JUAN [*to* THE MUSICIANS]. You will remain in this adjoining room. Understand? Now, as for the "Hallelujah Chorus": Remember, if something extraordinary should happen, an accident—for example, it might very well be that I might be swallowed up by Hell——

MUSICIAN. Sir??!——

DON JUAN. —simply go on playing. Understand? Keep on playing the "Hallelujah Chorus" until there's no one left in the room.

MUSICIAN. And our wages?

DON JUAN. Later! Later!

MUSICIAN. Later? When there's no one left in the room?

DON JUAN. Gentlemen, a true artist never worries about wages in advance. Where is your love of your art? Please, I beg of you: not another word about money! Don't destroy the deep feelings of respect which I have for all artists. [DON JUAN *bows very ceremoniously;* THE MUSICIANS *do likewise and withdraw into the neighboring room.* DON JUAN, *removing his gloves, inspects the table.*] Not bad!

LEPORELLO. I'm afraid the wine won't last, sir. Just a tiny glass for each guest——

DON JUAN. That will do. I have a hunch they will lose their taste for wine—at least, when the stone guest arrives.

LEPORELLO. Sir——

DON JUAN. Everything, my dear Leporello, looks wonderful —the shining silverware, the glittering glasses in the wavering candlelight. All my sweethearts, they'll choke with

46

envy when they see how a blasphemer lives, how magnificently a murderer can entertain! And, of course, they need never know that all the silverware is simply rented.

LEPORELLO. And that we can't pay for it——

DON JUAN. Envy is powerful, my dear Leporello; it alone can awaken what I need—their hope for the future, their trust in the judgment of Heaven. [*The doorbell rings.*]

LEPORELLO. Sir!——

DON JUAN. Where are the placecards?

LEPORELLO. You don't really believe he'll come here, do you, the one with the granite pedestal?

DON JUAN. Do *you* really think so?

LEPORELLO. Me?——

LEPORELLO *attempts a scornful laugh, which dies in his throat as the bell rings a second time.* DON JUAN *starts to put out the placecards.*

DON JUAN. If it is the veiled lady again, tell her I never—on principle—received veiled ladies. I know her. She wants to save my soul, hoping to entice me in this way to seduce her. Tell her we are well acquainted with this trick.

LEPORELLO *goes out fearfully.* THE MUSICIANS *offstage begin to tune up—a strange commingling of various melodies—while* DON JUAN *lays out the placecards; sometimes, reading a name, he cannot place it and shrugs. At last, he has one card left; this he burns in the candle flame.*

DON JUAN. You, the dead, more living than all the rest combined—you will not come—you, whom I embraced and did not recognize, and now that I do recognize you, all that I love has turned to ashes: your mouth, which I kissed, and the sparkle of your eyes behind your veil—ashes, like these——

LEPORELLO *returns.*

LEPORELLO. The Bishop of Cordoba!

DON JUAN. Blow these ashes off the table and tell the Bishop of Cordoba that he will have to wait a moment. But tell him politely! This Bishop isn't exactly a religious man—not that I blame him. However, I can use him. Remember, Leporello, without the Church there is no Hell.

LEPORELLO. Sir——

DON JUAN. Why are you shaking like that?

LEPORELLO. Sir—enough is enough, sir, don't push things too far—I mean, to invite a gravestone to dinner! I must say—an absolute dead man, who has been dead and mouldering since—well, what I mean to say, sir, is: I'm as big a rascal as the next fellow, as long as it pays off —I'll do anything if the price is right, mind you—on my honor, I'm no coward, but yesterday in the graveyard, sir —inviting a *statue* to dinner! No, sir, count me out. Enough is enough—God knows, I pissed on the base of the Commander's statue, but——

From behind the curtain comes a VOICE.

VOICE. Don Juan!

LEPORELLO. Holy Joseph and Mary!

DON JUAN. One moment.

LEPORELLO. He's coming! He's coming!

VOICE. Don Juan, dost thou hear me?

DON JUAN. "Just a minute!" I said.

LEPORELLO *falls on his knees.*

LEPORELLO. I am innocent. Mercy, I beg of you! I have a family—God in Heaven—five children and a wife. Mercy! I'll run all the way to the graveyard and wash off your tombstone, I swear it—with soap! Mercy!

LEPORELLO *races out.* DON JUAN *steps to the curtain in the background.*

DON JUAN. What's the matter back here? [CELESTINA *steps out.*] Why aren't you wearing all the stuff?

CELESTINA. The helmet's too tight.

DON JUAN. No one will pay any attention to that.

CELESTINA. I will!

DON JUAN. The ladies will be too excited either to see or think—that's the whole point of those theatrical performances they adore so.

CELESTINA. I've been thinking it over——

DON JUAN. What?

CELESTINA. A thousand pesos, or I won't go through with it.

DON JUAN. We agreed on five hundred!

CELESTINA. You can say what you like: It's still a blasphemy against God—and for that my price is a thousand, my lord, take it or leave it.

DON JUAN. Celestina!

CELESTINA. Business is business. A thousand is my rock-bottom price. And if I marry you off to the Duchess of Ronda, I want another thousand, I remind you—cash on the table!

DON JUAN *tears something from his neck.*

DON JUAN. Here! Now—disappear!

CELESTINA. An amulet?

DON JUAN. The last one I have. From my sainted mother. Now, disappear—go on!

CELESTINA. Stop pushing.

DON JUAN. Hurry up—please!

CELESTINA. It's not my fault, Don Juan, that you are bankrupt. Why don't you want to even hear my offer? You would be richer than the Bishop of Cordoba. I'm telling you: a castle with forty-four rooms——

DON JUAN. I don't want to hear any more about it!

CELESTINA. But now is the time, Don Juan.

DON JUAN. Will you please spare me your damned meddling matchmaking! I told the Commander, all Spain knows it, and I tell you for the last time: I will never get married!

CELESTINA. Many a man has said that.

DON JUAN. Oh, shut up!

DON JUAN *forces* CELESTINA *back behind the curtain, but it is only the terrified* LEPORELLO *who re-enters.*

DON JUAN. What's the matter?

LEPORELLO. Sir—I've forgotten, sir, what I'm supposed to say to the Bishop. . . . He is so stately, sir, and strides through the halls as if he can't wait to see the Heavens destroy us.

DON JUAN. Tell him I will be happy to receive him now.

LEPORELLO *goes out, leaving the swinging doors open.* DON JUAN, *preparing himself to receive* THE BISHOP, *draws a large armchair to the side, practices just how and where he will kneel, then nods to* THE MUSICIANS. *They begin to play a religious-sounding air.* DON JUAN *stands before the mirror, straightening his ruffles, while through the open door* THE VEILED LADY *enters slowly; he sees her in the mirror and starts, without turning around.*

THE LADY. Why are you afraid?

DON JUAN. Because I know that you are not Donna Anna—

for Donna Anna is dead. Why this veil? [*He turns around.*] Who are you?

THE LADY. You refused to see me. Then, suddenly, I found this door open.

DON JUAN. What can I do for you?

THE LADY. I know you, Juan. You can't do anything for me. That's just what's wrong with you. I loved you once because chess—the game of intellect—enticed you more than women did. And because you walked out on me like a man with a goal in life. I don't know whether you still have that goal. It was geometry. Now I see only your life as it is, Juan: full of women, but no geometry.

DON JUAN [*looks her over*]. Who are you? [*He tries to lift her veil.*]

THE LADY. Stop! [*He steps back.*] I am the Duchess of Ronda.

DON JUAN. Black as death, Duchess—that's how you entered my mirror—nothing should be that black. Women remind me of death—the more beautiful, the more deadly. Maybe that's why I can't stand women. Not to say, mind you, that I hate them.

THE LADY. I am dressed in black because I'm a widow.

DON JUAN. Through me?

THE LADY. No.

DON JUAN. Well, then—what is it you want, Duchess of Ronda?

THE LADY. I want to save you.

DON JUAN. Ah, yes—you are the lady who wants to marry me.

THE LADY. Juan, I see no other escape for you.

DON JUAN. Your perseverance is astonishing, Duchess of Ronda. And, of course, you're quite right: Although chess, the game of intellect, entices me more irresistibly than any woman, my life is full of women. And yet you're mistaken about one thing. No woman has ever conquered me, Duchess of Ronda, and I would rather go straight to Hell than to be married——

THE LADY. If there *were* such a place as Hell.

DON JUAN. Still—I know what I want.

THE LADY. Juan, you misunderstand me. I have not come as a woman seeking a husband. I have had more men than

I knew what to do with, overflowing with smiles, and one
of them, who thought he couldn't live without my smiles,
made me his Duchess, and then he died——

Don Juan. I see.

The Lady. Now I have this castle in Ronda. . . . And so
I thought: You could live in the left wing; I could go on
living in the right wing—there's a big courtyard in between. Quiet fountains, you know, with cooing doves and
the like. And actually, there would be no need for our
ever meeting—even if we wanted to, you understand. And
then with this there would be a sort of ducal power—
perhaps not great enough to completely wipe out your
stupid guilt, but great enough to silence the courts of the
world which accuse you of murder. To put it in so many
words—as long as you live in Ronda, no one will ever disturb you in your geometry.

Don Juan. But . . . ?

The Lady. No "but."

Don Juan. Your understanding of men, I'll grant you, is
extraordinary. But what will this salvation cost me?

The Lady. I want you to take a wife, Juan.

Don Juan. Enough!

The Lady. It may be, I still love you, but you needn't be
afraid—I have learned I don't need you to be happy, and
that above all is what I can offer you, my friend: I am
free of the illusion that I can't live without you. [*Pause.*]
Think it over. [*Pause.*] You are a man—you have always
simply loved yourself, Juan, and yet you have never found
yourself. So you hate us. You have always thought of us
as women, never as wives; each of us was an episode, but
an episode that somehow became involved with your
whole life. So you fear us. Why don't you put your faith
in a wife—whoever she may be—just once? It's the only
path, Juan, to your masculine geometry.

Leporello *shows in* The Bishop of Cordoba.

Leporello. His Eminence!

Don Juan. Ah—you will forgive me, Duchess of Ronda, His
Eminence and I must talk business, but I hope to see you
soon at dinner: unveiled!

The Lady. In Ronda, Juan, or nowhere.

The Lady *draws her cloak about her, makes a deep curtsy*

before THE BISHOP, *and goes out hurriedly, followed by*
LEPORELLO, *who closes the door.*

DON JUAN. You see how it is, Your Eminence—I don't have
a moment's peace. They all come with this fixed idea:
They must marry me. Do you believe in it?—I mean, that
a man and a woman, if they live under the same roof, can
live as uprightly as—well, as a man of honor needs to in
order to bear himself . . . Oh, I'm sorry, I almost forgot.
[*He kneels.*]

THE BISHOP. Rise!

DON JUAN. For twelve years, Eminence, the Spanish Church
has pursued me. I don't kneel out of force of habit; I kneel
in the very real hope that you have come here ready to
deal with a blasphemer whom you have been trying to
destroy in vain.

THE BISHOP. Rise! [THE BISHOP *turns to the table in order
to ease his embarrassment and picks up a roll, more from
uneasiness than hunger.*] What do you want from me?

DON JUAN *rises and brushes off his knees.*

DON JUAN. In a word: I want you to help me create a myth.

THE BISHOP. A—what?

DON JUAN. Will His Eminence be seated?

THE BISHOP. To create a myth?

DON JUAN. We don't have much time, Your Eminence—
the ladies will soon be here. So, with your permission, I
will not beat around the bush.

THE BISHOP. Please don't.

DON JUAN. My proposition is sincere and quite simple: Don
Juan Tenorio—your national archenemy who stands here
before you in the full glory of his manhood and on the
point of immortality, on the point of becoming, let's face
it, a legend—Don Juan Tenorio is determined and ready
to die—this very day!

THE BISHOP. To die?

DON JUAN. Under certain conditions.

THE BISHOP. Such as . . . ?

DON JUAN. Speaking frankly (we're quite alone, Your
Eminence): You, the Spanish Church, will give me a
modest income, nothing further, a cell in a monastery—
not *too* tiny a cell, mind you, and if possible with a view

of the mountains of Andalusia—there let me live with a little bread and wine, nameless, safe from women, quiet and peaceful, with my geometry. And to you, Bishop of Cordoba, I offer what the Church of Spain wants and needs more than money itself: the legend of the blasphemer's descent into Hell. [DON JUAN *offers him a tray.*] What do you say?

THE BISHOP. Thank you very much.

DON JUAN. That is caviar, Your Eminence.

THE BISHOP. So I see.

DON JUAN *takes a bite himself and puts the tray back down;*
THE BISHOP *seats himself.*

DON JUAN. Something is going to have to happen, Your Eminence! For twelve years now, this monument has been standing there with its terrible motto: May Heaven destroy the blasphemer! And I, the blasphemer, go walking past it every day, as often as I like, as undestroyed as any man in Seville. How long can this go on? Seduction and murder, laughter and mockery, and nothing happens, nothing at all!—— [DON JUAN *perches on the edge of the table.*] Don't you see? This simply cannot go on! [THE BISHOP *is silent.*] Understand me correctly, Bishop, I am not simply tired of women; I am spiritually tired—tired of blasphemy. Twelve years of irredeemable destiny because of a childlike challenge on a morning of blue skies and sunlight! I have really hoped that something *would* happen to me. Don't smile! I have believed that somehow, someday, Heaven would be heard from. . . . But, as you yourself have seen, Your Eminence, my blasphemy has simply made me famous, particularly as a seducer of women—an activity which unfortunately (at least, in the best circles) sometimes involves the killing of husbands. "Unfortunately," I say, for several times, when I was on the point of it, the ladies returned to the arms of their husbands—a fate worse than death. . . .

THE BISHOP. You are thinking of the worthy Lopez——

DON JUAN. I mention no names, Your Eminence.

THE BISHOP. Don Balthazar Lopez.

DON JUAN. For thirty-three years I have shared the fate of all famous men: All the world knows our deeds, but no

one knows our souls. I shudder when I hear people talk
about me—as though I ever pursued women!

THE BISHOP. Nevertheless——

DON JUAN. At first, I'll grant you, it was fun. My hands, they
said, were like divining rods—able to find what husbands
had never found in ten years of searching for the springs
of pleasure. And Lord knows what else! Perhaps you know
yourself, Your Eminence, how wearisome time becomes as
you see their enraptured mouths babbling of happiness.
Oh, it's flattering to us the first hundred times, perhaps,
but—the more womanish a man seems to himself, the
more irresistible he seems to women! Or so it seems. And
all that is certainly no occupation for a man, not to speak
of a profession!

THE BISHOP. Nevertheless, you couldn't leave it alone——

DON JUAN. It was so much easier to do it, Your Eminence,
than to try to talk the women out of it. At least, in my
case. And you, my dear Bishop, have done more than anyone else to increase my unholy fame. The ladies leave
your sermons dreaming of me, and their husbands are
ready to draw their swords before I have even glanced
their way. So I have to fight everywhere I go; I'm always
dueling somebody. The result? Practice makes perfect;
so that now I scarcely have time to resheathe my bloody
sword before the widow is hanging on my neck, sobbing,
and I am consoling her. What else is there for me, then—
what else appropriate to my fame—than to become a victim of my fame? Notice, incidentally, how no one in our
chivalrous Spain talks about the way women transgress
against *me!*—unless I simply leave the widow lying there,
turn on my heel, and go my own way—which is not quite
so simple, Your Eminence! We know the relentless vengeance of the woman who had *hoped* to be seduced, in
vain—— [DON JUAN, *who has been pacing to and fro,
now sees that* THE BISHOP *is more interested in the table
than in his conversation, and stops.*] If you like my caviar,
Bishop, please help yourself, but pay attention to what
I'm saying!

THE BISHOP. Why do you look at me like that?

DON JUAN. Extraordinary . . . For the first time, I see you
close at hand, Bishop. I remember lifting a curtain over a

window once and seeing you pass by in the midst of a procession. You were much fatter, then.

THE BISHOP. My predecessor, no doubt.

DON JUAN. And nevertheless I have the feeling I know your
shadowy face. Remarkable! Where have we seen each
other before?

THE BISHOP *stands*.

THE BISHOP. Marriages shamed, families destroyed, daugh-
ters seduced, fathers murdered, not to mention the husbands who must survive their disgrace—and you, who are
guilty of all this, dare speak of your own problems!

DON JUAN. Why not?

THE BISHOP. Do you have any idea what it is like to be
laughed at by everyone in the country as a cuckolded husband?

DON JUAN. Do you, Your Eminence?

THE BISHOP. A man like this worthy Lopez——

DON JUAN. You seem almost to be in some sort of league
with him, Your Eminence, the way you keep mentioning
him, your worthy Lopez, who has given half his fortune
to aid the Spanish Church in its persecution of me—to
which it is so devoted as to surround my house with its
own agents! You grow pale, Your Eminence, but it's true:
I can no longer even go out for a walk without having to
stick somebody with my sword. It *is* a problem, Your
Eminence, believe me, a real problem. I am weary of killing. [LEPORELLO *enters*.] Don't disturb us now! [LEPO-
RELLO *withdraws again*.]

THE BISHOP. To come back to business——

DON JUAN. You need only say "Yes," Bishop, and the myth
is made. I have a person ready to play the part of the dead
Commander. The ladies will shriek the moment they hear
his voice. Don't worry about a thing. A sneering laugh
from me, an explosion at the right moment, so that the
ladies hide their eyes—notice, Your Eminence, this clever
machine under the table—and suddenly the room stinks
of sulphur and smoke. The ladies are more fearful for
their own lives than they are concerned about me. All
this very fast, you understand—surprise is the mother of
miracles. Then you, I think, had better speak a few

words, which will intensify the effect—my musicians strike
up the "Hallelujah Chorus"—and: curtain!

THE BISHOP. And you?

DON JUAN. In the cellar, Your Eminence; you see this
cleverly concealed trap door? Naturally, not without an
appropriate scream—one which will, according to Aris-
totle's recipe, arouse pity and terror. In the cellar I have
a monk's robe and a sharp knife with which to cut off my
famous mustache. Call me Brother Leon or whatever you
will, Your Eminence, and, believe me, I will be a monk
such as you have never seen before—I sense it!

THE BISHOP. Hm.

DON JUAN. I am full of humility when I see the stars; I know
no higher joy than in contemplating this manifestation of
a harmonious spirit. Believe me, Your Eminence! What
else have I ever longed for but the pure, the clear, the
translucent—the true!

THE BISHOP. Hm.

DON JUAN. One condition: We both guard the secret; otherwise, it won't be worth the trouble, obviously. My descent
into Hell (as rumor is bound to describe it, not to mention our poets) will console the ladies, their husbands, the
threatening mob of my disciples—in short, everyone will
be satisfied in his own way, and we will be giving our
century what it so desperately needs: something surpris-
ing, something positive—a myth.

THE BISHOP. Hm.

DON JUAN. You understand: Don Juan, the seducer and
mocker, is dead. I have my peace in geometry, and you,
Your Eminence, have an incomparable master stroke, an
obvious and fresh testimonial to the justice of Heaven,
such as you will otherwise never find in all Spain!

THE BISHOP. I understand . . .

LEPORELLO *enters again.*

LEPORELLO. Sir . . .

DON JUAN. What now?

LEPORELLO. The ladies are here.

DON JUAN. Where?

LEPORELLO. In the patio. And rather excited, sir. They're
all thinking: Don Juan and I, tête-à-tête, and so on. In
fact, if I hadn't slammed and locked the door, there

wouldn't be *any* of them here. All that fluttering and cackling—like an Andalusian henhouse!

DON JUAN. Good.

LEPORELLO. Which is to say, the way my master likes it. But right now everything is quiet; they're all watching each other out of the corners of their eyes from behind their fans.

DON JUAN. Show them in. [*After a glance at* THE BISHOP.] Let's say—in three minutes. [LEPORELLO *goes out.*] Your Eminence, tell me the name of my monastery.

THE BISHOP. You are very sure of yourself, Don Juan.

DON JUAN. Naturally, the Church can only make use of a successful legend; I understand your fear, Your Eminence. But rest assured; the story is credible and in no way original; it's an ancient theme—a statue which strikes down the murderer—you find it throughout classical antiquity—and, as for a theme like the mocking of a death's-head which in turn drags the mocker into eternity, note some of the Breton ballads our soldiers sing. And, even if our little production only partially succeeds, the Spanish Church will not hesitate to nurture and protect my legend, to defend it from all suspicions. The ends sanctify the means. Never fear, Bishop, I know the Spanish Church!

THE BISHOP. And you know me, too?——

THE BISHOP *takes off his bishop's mitre and his black-rimmed spectacles.* DON JUAN *steps back.*

DON JUAN. Lopez?

LOPEZ. Don Balthazar Lopez.

DON JUAN. So that's how it is.

LOPEZ. We saw each other once, Don Juan, just for a fleeting moment. A white curtain blew into the candle flame, remember? You were with my wife. A sudden tongue of red fire—I had to rush in and extinguish it——

DON JUAN. Correct.

LOPEZ. There wasn't time to fight.

DON JUAN. Let me see now—what was your wife's name?

LOPEZ. Today is my day of vengeance, whether you remember her name or not. Oh, I know well enough that you didn't seduce my wife.

DON JUAN. You do?

LOPEZ. She seduced you.

DON JUAN. What do you want in my house?

LOPEZ. Now that I have discovered what you are secretly
planning in order to escape our revenge, let the ladies
enter; it will be a pleasure for me to unmask your blasphemous plot. You have miscalculated, my lord; you are
going to remain on this earth just like the rest of us, and
I will not rest until I accomplish my revenge—here on
this earth—in short, until I see you too, Don Juan, as a
husband!

DON JUAN. Ha!

LOPEZ. Yes—married! And to my wife!

DON JUAN. You miserable cur . . . [DON JUAN *draws his
sword.*] And suppose you too have miscalculated? The
people are very credulous, and Spain has already banished
many a man for unmasking a legend. I warn you, Don
Balthazar Lopez, it can be a very dangerous thing to
speak the truth.

LOPEZ. What's the meaning of this sword?

DON JUAN. You too are very sure of yourself——

LOPEZ. I'm not the Bishop—that's all there is to it. What
good is this legend to you without the eventual refuge in
a monastery? No matter where you go, your very appearance refutes the story of a descent into Hell—you remain
Don Juan forever, Don Juan the accursed, the weary—
and there's no escape.

DON JUAN. And if I simply kill you now?

LOPEZ. You know the answer yourself.

DON JUAN. What?

LOPEZ. That that too will afford you no escape from this
world. [DON JUAN *resheathes his sword.*] The game is over,
my friend.

LEPORELLO *appears.*

LEPORELLO. The ladies!

LOPEZ. Even a master chess player, it seems, may just once
overconfidently pick up the wrong piece—and suddenly
find himself in checkmate.

THE LADIES *burst in, a babble of noisy indignation; they
pause and fall silent before the seeming Bishop (LOPEZ has
put his bishop's mitre back on); they kiss the hem of his
robe. Then:*

DONNA ELVIRA. Your Eminence, we have been deceived!

DONNA BELISA. Shamelessly betrayed!

DONNA ELVIRA. I thought he was at death's door—otherwise I would never have come—I, the Commander's widow!

DONNA ISABEL. None of us would!

DONNA ELVIRA. Look how he stands there. The murderer of my husband. I am simply speechless. Speechless. Why did I ever accept such an invitation? I am a lady, Your Eminence——

DONNA BELISA. And I suppose *we're* not?

THE BISHOP. Donna Belisa——

DONNA BELISA. Aren't we ladies, Your Eminence?

THE BISHOP. Calm yourself, Donna Belisa. I am well aware that you are the wife of the worthy Lopez——

DONNA BELISA. Don't mention his name!

THE BISHOP. Why not?

DONNA BELISA. The worthy Lopez—as he always calls himself—not once did he ever fight for me; all the other husbands at least fought. I believe I'm the only one in this whole group who isn't a widow——

THE BISHOP. Calm yourself.

DONNA ELVIRA. You don't suppose, Your Eminence, that he—the murderer of my husband—thinks to marry me, with your blessing, or anything equally horrible?

THE LADIES. Marry? You?

DONNA ELVIRA. I was the first, after all——

THE BISHOP. Ladies! Ladies!

DONNA ELVIRA. I had thought, Your Eminence, he had wanted to beg my forgiveness. What else? I was ready for anything, Your Eminence, but not for this parade of overdressed adventuresses who seem to think I am one of them!

THE LADIES. Ah!

DONNA ELVIRA. Never mind, you pack of hypocrites, I know what you are doing in this house.

DONNA BELISA. And you, madam?

DONNA ELVIRA. I have come to forgive. [*To* THE BISHOP.] Ask the priest, Gabriel Téllez, who is my confessor. [*To* THE LADIES.] And now where is he, your beloved—? you geese, who are always dreaming of him—! let me at him, so I can scratch out his eyes!

DON JUAN *steps forward.*

DON JUAN. Here I am. [*Silence.*] I am delighted, my darlings, that you have all come. The group is not quite complete, I fear, but enough to celebrate the instability of love. [*Indignation.*] Ladies, please remember—once, we loved each other! [*One of them spits at his feet.*] I am astonished, Donna Viola, to see how little remains of our tender passion.

DONNA ISABEL. My name isn't Viola.

DON JUAN. Pardon me.

DONNA VIOLA. He calls her Viola. I can't stand it.

DON JUAN. How fleeting are all emotions, which—in the very moment we feel them—bring us so close to eternity we are blinded to individual names and persons. Yes, Donna Fernanda, it's a terrible thing!

DONNA ISABEL. My name is also not Fernanda.

DON JUAN. My dear——

DONNA ISABEL. That's what you call all of them: "My dear"!

DON JUAN. I didn't mean it personally, Donna Isabel—ah, now I remember: Donna Isabel, you with the boundless soul, which was always overflowing; why didn't you sob all the time like the others? [*To* THE BISHOP.] You are right—the memory of man is most peculiar; afterwards, there's always something unbelievable about an event— we only know immediacy: a white curtain blowing into a candle flame . . .

DONNA BELISA. Oh God!

DON JUAN. Another time, there was a rustling in the reeds, where I crouched, afraid, my sword drawn; it was only a wild duck in the moonlight.

DONNA VIOLA. Oh God!

DON JUAN. What I remember are objects: a tasteless vase, slippers, a porcelain crucifix. And, frequently, odors: the perfume of fading myrtles——

DONNA FERNANDA. Oh God!

DON JUAN. And so on. And far in the distant landscape of my youth—I hear it yet—the baying of the hounds in a moonlit park——

DONNA ELVIRA. Oh God!

DONNA INEZ. Oh God!

DON JUAN. And yet I can't remember the names—scarcely

even the faces. In the end, they all melt into one face—which I no longer recognize by daylight. [*All* The Ladies *have covered their faces.*] So it is. I have no recollections of nights with women. I have passed through life without a trace, like a shimmer on the water. And when some youngster asks me: "What's it like, being with a woman?" I don't know what to answer, honestly. I don't remember, any more than I remember my birth. Only, when it recurs again, then I know: "Ah, yes—*this* is what it was like, always." And then all that remains is a sad smile, a smile, because once again we have sought and failed to find the impossible: permanence. [The Ladies *let their hands fall slowly.*] And yet, my darlings, can we really say we regret any of it? [*Indignation.*] Donna Belisa?

Donna Belisa. You shameless wretch!

Don Juan. Donna Viola?

Donna Viola. Villain!

Don Juan. Donna Fernanda, do you have any regrets?

Donna Fernanda. Beast!

Don Juan. Donna Isabel?

Donna Isabel. You disgust me!

Don Juan. Donna Inez?

Donna Inez. Monster!

Don Juan. And you—the most mature of them all—Donna Elvira?

Donna Elvira. I am simply speechless . . . [Don Juan *gestures toward the table.*]

Don Juan. Shall we sit down?

They all seat themselves.

Donna Elvira. And you, Your Eminence, are you going to permit all this? You hear how these ladies of Seville are scorned and insulted and you haven't a word to say? Is it true then that there is no Heaven that protects virtue and punishes the blasphemous? Is this true, Bishop of Cordoba?

The Bishop. I am not the Bishop of Cordoba. [*He throws off his bishop's robes.*] My name is Lopez.

Donna Belisa. You??!

Lopez. Don Balthazar Lopez.

Don Juan. Chancellor of the Exchequer, from Toledo, if I mistake not, possessor of various honors and medals, as you can see. Señor Lopez has suddenly taken upon himself this rather ticklish job of defending the jealousy of husbands.

LOPEZ. Your mockery is at an end, Don Juan. [To THE LADIES.] He will not leave this house, ladies, not until he has received his just punishment. I have seen to it. At every door that leads from this infamous house a naked sword awaits him. [To DON JUAN.] The hour of judgment is here, my friend, the cup of your blasphemy is full to overflowing!

DON JUAN. Hasn't it been for quite some time? And still nothing happens—it's a popular joke in Seville. Yesterday, in the cemetery, Leporello, didn't we try in every possible way to insult the dead Commander?

LEPORELLO. I am innocent, ladies! I have five children and a wife—I——

DON JUAN. Didn't I invite him here to dinner?

DONNA ELVIRA. My husband??!

DON JUAN. My worthy servant not only defamed the base of his statue—in a manner that I hesitate to mention—but also maintains that the statue nodded its stone head— evidently as a sign that he was free to accept a dinner invitation tonight.

LOPEZ. Calm yourselves, ladies!

DON JUAN. Why doesn't he come, then, this commander of Heaven's battalions? What more can I do, my dears, to get him to fulfill his promise by destroying me?

LOPEZ. Where are you going, Donna Elvira?

DONNA ELVIRA. I feel faint. I can't see him, I can't . . .

LOPEZ. Stay, Donna Elvira, stay. [To all of them.] Don't let yourselves be made fools of, ladies! Listen to me! None of this is true—it's all a practical joke—listen to me! I don't know who is hiding here to feign the Commander's voice, but I know and I proclaim it before all the world: Here, somewhere in this room, there is a person concealed, placed there by this gentleman, and that person is to play the part of the Commander! Yes—play the part! A person, I say, who is too far beneath contempt for Don Balthazar Lopez to trouble himself with!

VOICE. That is not true!

LOPEZ. But as for *this* gentleman . . .

VOICE. That is not true.

LOPEZ. Silence!

VOICE. I will not be insulted, and least of all by you, Don Balthazar Lopez. I know you of old . . .

THE LADIES *have leaped up from their chairs.*

LOPEZ. Calm yourselves, ladies! Here, see with your own eyes—this cunning machine concealed beneath the table. An explosion and clouds of sulphur are to throw you into a panic, so that you lose your reason and believe that Don Juan has been swallowed up by Hell. A judgment of Heaven, which is nothing but theatre, a mockery of God, designed to found a legend which would enable him to escape our revenge and to make fools out of all Spain!— this was his plan, ladies, nothing more! [*To* DON JUAN.] Do you deny it?

DON JUAN. Not at all.

LOPEZ. You hear him, ladies!

DON JUAN. Nothing but theatre. That's what I've been saying for twelve years: There's really no Hell, no Other World, no Judgment of Heaven. Señor Lopez is absolutely right: nothing but theatre. What else should it be? [*He throws open the curtains in the background.*] Here . . .

The purported statue is, at first glance, by no means unimpressive. THE LADIES *disperse in panic.*

DONNA ELVIRA. My husband . . . ? What *is* this?! I thought you were in Heaven, that you had heard my confessions! For old time's sake. But haven't you gotten over it yet in eternity? I have decorated your monument with flowers faithfully—for it's nobody's business what our marriage was really like! Enough of that! I have forgiven you, my dear, so if Heaven has sent you to talk over our marriage again—wait until we're in private, at least—not here.

DONNA ELVIRA *draws her cape about her and rushes out; the other* LADIES *stand as if paralyzed;* THE MUSICIANS *start to play the "Hallelujah Chorus."*

LEPORELLO. Look, he's stretching out his arm!

LOPEZ. Nothing but theatre!

LEPORELLO. Look!

DON JUAN. Look, all of you. See how I take his hand, so that

he can pull me down to Hell—tell this tale throughout the
land, I beg of you.

LEPORELLO. Help!——

DON JUAN. Look, all of you——

LEPORELLO. Help!

DON JUAN. —and go in peace!

LEPORELLO. My salary, sir, what about my salary?

An explosion. Smoke billows up. DON JUAN *and the statue
sink through the floor—all very theatrical.*

LOPEZ. This is not true, ladies!—get up!—don't kneel!—it's
all a trick! I swear it! He will never leave this house, I've
seen to that, not without the punishment he deserves!

THE LADIES *kneel;* THE THREE COUSINS *rush in, with drawn
swords.*

A COUSIN. What happened?

LOPEZ. What the devil—— Why didn't you stay at the
doors?

A COUSIN. Where is he?

LEPORELLO. Gone to the Devil.

LOPEZ. That's not true!! [THE THREE COUSINS *cross themselves and kneel.*] I don't care if all Seville believes this, we
will find him, my dove—and he will have you yet!

LOPEZ *drags his sobbing wife out violently; everyone is kneeling and murmuring prayers, as*

The curtain falls.

INTERMEZZO

CELESTINA, *with hat and umbrella, followed by* LEPORELLO, *appears before the curtain.*

CELESTINA. I want to talk to her in private.

LEPORELLO. And me?

CELESTINA. Go down and wait by the carriage until I'm through here. Oh, I know you! A little taste of a convent garden, the ringing of the vesper bells—and you go all to pieces. The next thing I know, you'll be believing, yourself, that he's in Hell! I see through you! Purely and simply because you're worried about the salary he owes you. Men have no character; once you get to worrying about your money, you're ready to believe what everyone else in the world believes. [A NUN *appears.*] Evaporate. [LEPORELLO *exits.*] Sister Elvira?

SISTER ELVIRA. God bless you, madam.

CELESTINA. I must have a word with you in private. I have come here, Sister Elvira, because I have a bad conscience. Because of the past, you understand. I can't free myself from the painful thought that you are here in this shabby old convent, eating barley soup and praying all day long, simply because of me—no one but me!

SISTER ELVIRA. The convent is my peace and poverty is my reward——

CELESTINA. That's what you wrote me, I know. And that your soul grows ever more free while you eat your barley soup. I know all about that; I was brought up on barley soup. And that you are in the process of turning into a totally spiritual being.

SISTER ELVIRA. That is so.

CELESTINA. Well, it's none of my affair, but whenever I pass your former palace in Seville and think of you here in poverty—simply because you were taken in by that hoax about the stone statue—believe me, Sister Elvira, I can't keep from reproaching myself!

65

SISTER ELVIRA. "A hoax," you call it? When a poor creature who has allowed herself to be deceived by vain illusions all her life finally has her eyes opened?

CELESTINA. Sister Elvira, I honestly never thought anyone would believe it—so help me—and now, just look, all Spain believes it! So much so, that a person doesn't dare to speak the truth in public any more. This poor miserable Lopez! Have you heard? Banished from the country, simply because he dared to insist that the whole thing had been a hoax. And now, they say, he's gone and hanged himself over in Morocco——

SISTER ELVIRA. Don Balthazar Lopez?

CELESTINA. Men! That's all I can say. First he gives half his fortune to the Church—for years, he'd been the cheapest customer I ever had—and then he doesn't have nerve enough to know the truth and keep his mouth shut. So now everyone says: "You see? He has hanged himself, like Judas in the wilderness."

SISTER ELVIRA. May God have mercy on his soul.

CELESTINA. Sister Elvira, at least you ought to know: I was the hoaxer who played the part of the statue—I, no one but I! You mustn't simply shake your head like that, Sister Elvira. I've taken three hours out of my business day to travel all the way here and tell you the straight truth, and, whether you believe me or not, I tell you, I did it for money—nothing more, so help me; I don't want to do you any harm, but when I read your letters and I see this deep sorrow and mourning that I have caused, I naturally reproach myself bitterly. And frankly, speaking as a woman, I can't bear to see you creeping through life on your knees just because of a man. "No!" I said to my girl. "Lock up the place. Today we're going to visit this nun; I'm the last eyewitness to this affair." I know for a fact: Don Juan is not in Hell. Believe me, Sister Elvira, your prayers are a waste of time. Sister Elvira, I've seen him— with my own eyes! All your magnanimity is for the birds believe me, and it doesn't make any difference how much —you understand me? Hell has nothing to do with it, barley soup you eat! [She listens to THE NUN's murmuring voice.] Agent of Judas? Me? [She takes up her umbrella resolutely.] Very well. Just as you wish. Fine. If it helps you, Madam, to think he's in Hell simply because he doesn't want anything more to do with you . . . fine! I don't have time to waste on people who can't even believe the word of an eyewitness. Good! Fine!

The vesper bells begin to ring.

SISTER ELVIRA. Listen, madam! Don't you hear?

CELESTINA. What?

SISTER ELVIRA. How he calls to me to pray for him? Never has he been sweeter, never dearer to me than now, when he is in Hell, burning in eternal flames—oh, never have I loved a man as I do now, in forgiving him——

CELESTINA. Woman!

SISTER ELVIRA. Oh, I forgive . . . I forgive . . . [SISTER ELVIRA *wanders out, following the vesper bells.*]

CELESTINA. And for this I took off three hours in the middle of a working day! God forgive us all! [*She crosses herself.*]

LEPORELLO *enters.*

LEPORELLO. Celestina, what are you doing?

CELESTINA. Getting converted.

LEPORELLO. What?

CELESTINA. Cross yourself. There's nothing to be done here. He is in Hell.

some reason or other and then she was very beautiful... You're quite right to remind me. She was very beautiful. [DON JUAN *has no time to waste.*] Do people always behave like this when they go to a theater? [DON JUAN *shrugs.*]

TERESA, *later also* DON JUAN *and* PRIEST, *with others.*

ACT FIVE

A loggia.

In the foreground: a table set for two. DON JUAN *is waiting, evidently for the other person; presently he becomes impatient and rings a small bell. A mute* SERVANT *enters.*

DON JUAN. I have given orders that I was not to be called from my work unless dinner was really ready. Now I've been waiting here for half an hour. As if my days aren't short enough! [THE SERVANT *looks sympathetic.*] I know, Alonzo, it's not your fault—— [DON JUAN *picks up a book.*] But where *is* she? [THE SERVANT *shrugs.*] All right. Thank you. [THE SERVANT *goes out.* DON JUAN *tries to interest himself in his book. Suddenly he flings it angrily into a corner and calls.*] Alonzo! When people are finally ready to eat, I'll be in my room!

Up from the garden comes the corpulent BISHOP OF COR-DOBA—*the former Father Diego—with an aster in his hand.*

THE BISHOP. Where are you off to in such a hurry?

DON JUAN. Ah!——

THE BISHOP. We were expecting you in the garden, my dear fellow. It's an enchanting evening out there. How I regret that I can't stay with you today! Over there, under the arcade, looking out across the gorge of Ronda, with the last sun on the gleaming asters—red and yellow and violet —then the green coolness of the valley, already lying in shadow—every time, I think to myself: Here is Paradise, lying at my feet.

DON JUAN. I know.

THE BISHOP. But now it's autumn. [*He sniffs at the red aster.*]

DON JUAN. A glass of wine, Diego?

THE BISHOP. Thank you. [DON JUAN *gives him an apéritif.*] I have even thought: Those ancient Moors, who built gardens like this—what a marvelous talent they must have had

for living life to the brim! All these courtyards, these cool
gentle zephyrs, vista upon vista, a silence not of the grave,
but rather full of the secrets of bluish distance seen
through a lacy latticework; one strolls about, refreshed by
the soft shadows, and yet the coolness is bright from the
mirror—like the reflection of a sunny wall—how delightful
and charming and—er—fleshly all this is! Not to mention
the fountains; what art, to let the praise of creation play
upon our senses—what mastery, to enjoy the impermanent
in flowing water—what culture! I have often thought:
The most important result of that war which we called
a crusade was that one day the victor must have perceived
what he'd been missing all his life, and at least learned
something from the vanquished. [DON JUAN *refills his
glass.*] The Duchess will be along any minute now.

DON JUAN. Let us hope.

THE BISHOP. She said she was not feeling too well. [*They
stand and drink.*] And how's the geometry coming along?

DON JUAN. Fine.

THE BISHOP. I've been thinking a great deal about what you
told me last time—the story about the dimensions, you
know, and how even geometry comes at last to a point
where you can no longer demonstrate its truth. Line, Surface, Space—but what is the fourth dimension? Eh? And
yet intellectually you can prove that it *must* exist—— [*He
breaks off, as* DON JUAN, *obviously not listening, is refilling
his own glass.*] Don Juan, what is wrong with you?

DON JUAN. With me? Nothing. What do you mean? Nothing
at all. [*He empties his glass.*] Nothing worth talking about.
[*He fills his glass a third time.*] Every day I ask specifically
not to be called until dinner is really ready. What's the
use? First it was the gong, which the Duchess didn't hear
if the crickets were chirping—so I had another one made,
which rang out over the whole damned valley—believe me,
all Ronda knew when dinner was served up here! Only the
Duchess didn't know. I ordered my servant to personally
seek out the Duchess and to personally inform her: Dinner
is served! And not to call me until the Duchess had actually crossed the courtyard. She laughed! It's pettiness,
I know, not worth mentioning—which is precisely why
it is such torture to me! What can I do? I'm her prisoner.

Really! Don't forget that! I don't dare leave this castle; if I'm seen out there, my legend is dead, which means I'll have to go back to being Don Juan . . . [*He tosses off the third glass.*] Let's not talk about it any more.

THE BISHOP. Excellent sherry.

DON JUAN. Oh, I'm sorry! [*He fills* THE BISHOP'S *glass again.*]

THE BISHOP. The Duchess is a wonderful woman. She is cheerful, yet clever; she knows very well that you, her husband, are not happy; and that is the only thing she regrets.

DON JUAN. She can do nothing about it, I know.

THE BISHOP. And yet . . . ?

DON JUAN. Every day when I enter this loggia I have the blazing feeling: I won't put up with it any more! It's silly, I know, but I won't put up with it. And when she finally comes, I act as though it really were too silly for words—we sit down, and I say, "Please pass the bread."

THE BISHOP. She loves you?

DON JUAN. That has nothing to do with it. If she spends a week in Seville having her hair dyed, I won't say that I actually miss her—and yet . . .

THE BISHOP. It is not good for man to live alone; that is why God created woman.

DON JUAN. And did He think then that everything would be fine? Seriously, the anger I feel toward a Creator who idiotically split us into Man and Woman grows stronger year by year—I taste it every night at the dinner table. What a horrible thing, that man is the only creation which is not single and entire, and the greater his longing becomes, the more accursed he is—forever cut off from the opposite sex! Oh, I should be thankful for this place, I know! I have only the choice, whether I want to be dead or whether I want to be here. Thankful for this prison in the Garden of Paradise!

THE BISHOP. And yet . . .

DON JUAN. It is a prison.

THE BISHOP. With forty-four rooms. Think of the poor, Don Juan, who have no roof to shelter them.

DON JUAN. I envy them.

THE BISHOP. Why?

DON JUAN. Because they may go insane and think no more. . . . Why couldn't I have been left in the monastery?

THE BISHOP. Not everyone can live in a monastery.

DON JUAN. "Multiply and be fruitful."

THE BISHOP. Thus it is written.

DON JUAN. No sword, no condemnation by the Church—as you well know—has ever made me tremble. But she, a woman who loves me, brings me to it every day. And why? I see that I can no longer laugh at the ridiculousness of life—a sort of paralysis, as though I had taken poison. I'm becoming satisfied, and yet there's no real satisfaction in that! She is a woman—the best of all conceivable women, perhaps, but still a woman, and I am a man. No matter. Even with the best of good will on both sides, it still becomes a wrestling match to see who manages to defeat the other—with the best of good will. Oh, you should see us, Bishop, when we're alone. No one raises his voice. We have brought it all down to a kind of murderous politeness. We express sorrow if our other half is not happy. What more do you want to make the prison complete? There's only one thing left—for Sex to really throw the noose around my neck and strangle me.

THE BISHOP. Meaning?

DON JUAN. For me to become a father. And what will I do then? Heaven knows, *she* can't help it. We will sit down at the table as though nothing had happened and say: "Please pass the bread."

MIRANDA, *the Duchess of Ronda, appears*; DON JUAN *and* THE BISHOP *drink.* MIRANDA *is prettier than ever—womanly maturity and natural modesty personified.*

MIRANDA. Am I interrupting?

THE BISHOP. Not at all, my dear Miranda. We were just chatting about Don Juan's descent into Hell. [*To* DON JUAN.] Have you seen the new play in Seville? [*To* MIRANDA.] It's playing now at the theatre.

DON JUAN. I never get into town.

MIRANDA. A play, you say?

THE BISHOP. "The Trickster of Seville," it's called, or "The Stone Guest." I went the other night—you see, it is thought that our prior, Gabriel Téllez, actually wrote it.

MIRANDA. How is it?

THE BISHOP. Good, very good. Not without a certain amount of humor. Don Juan actually descends into Hell, and the audience shudders and applauds. You really ought to see it, Juan.

DON JUAN. To see how I go to Hell?

THE BISHOP. What else is the theatre good for? The truth cannot be shown—only felt. Imagine an audience being shown the real Don Juan—here in this autumnal loggia in the Valley of Ronda! The ladies would plume themselves and say to their husbands on the way home: "You see?" And the husbands would rub their hands in secret glee: "The famous Don Juan in carpet slippers—just like us!" Yet there always comes a point where the unusual begins to seem all too usual. And then where—as my secretary would say—where is the punishment? Not to mention the silly laughter of our youngsters whose imaginations work so actively that, when it comes to a matter of life and death, they jump right out of their seats with excitement. Not to consider them would be a mistake! And some idiot, who likes to think of himself as a deep pessimist, would then explain: "You see, marriage—that's the true Hell." No, no, it's too horrible to imagine all the platitudes that would be coined by an audience exposed to nothing but reality. . . . God punishes man by creating him as he is, not as he ought to be, and the atonement for all that we have done in our pride and obstinacy is to learn to live, as we grow mature, with the knowledge: There is no solution! We must live with the necessity of our unfulfilled longing—as creatures of a creation that does not conform to our geometry—we must learn to live without cursing—for as long as we curse our fate, even the happiness we *might* have is only a purgatory—all this goes without saying, but only the legend can *show* it, the created figure of a Don Juan, the full spectacle of the Descent Into Hell. [*He holds out his hand to* MIRANDA.] Farewell, Duchess of Ronda.

MIRANDA. Are you really going?

THE BISHOP. I must, I must. [*He holds out his hand to* DON JUAN.] Farewell, Trickster of Seville.

DON JUAN. Will the play be published?

THE BISHOP. I've seen to it. The people enjoy it tremendously—seeing a man on the stage actually doing the things they secretly want to do, and finally paying for it; it comforts them in their own half-existence.

MIRANDA. But don't I appear in the play, Diego?

THE BISHOP. No.

MIRANDA. Thank God.

THE BISHOP. Nor do I—thank God even more—for otherwise we would have had to ban it, and Heaven knows the theatre needs all the good plays it can get. Nevertheless, I am very dubious as to whether it is really by Tirso de Molina; it's very regular, it seems to me, and stylistically far inferior to his other works. However . . . [*He puts his aster on the table.*] God bless your table!

THE BISHOP *goes out, accompanied by* DON JUAN. MIRANDA *is alone for a few moments; her expression shows that she does not feel well for a second. She sees the crumpled book on the floor.* DON JUAN *returns.*

MIRANDA. What happened to this book?

DON JUAN. Ah——

MIRANDA. Did you throw it into the corner?

DON JUAN. What's the matter with you?

MIRANDA. You asked if it were to be published. This is it— "The Trickster of Seville, or The Stone Guest."

DON JUAN. He must have sent it to us.

MIRANDA. And why did you throw it away? [DON JUAN *holds out her chair for her.*]

DON JUAN. It's time to eat.

They sit down in silence.

MIRANDA. You misunderstand me, Juan . . .

DON JUAN. Of course, my dear.

MIRANDA. I—I'm going to have to lie down for a minute.

DON JUAN. Do you want some wine?

MIRANDA. Thank you, no.

DON JUAN. Why not?

MIRANDA. It's nothing. Suddenly I felt so dizzy. Juan—I think we're going to have a child.

DON JUAN. A child—— [THE SERVANT *appears in the door.*] So. We have come this far. [THE SERVANT *goes.*]

MIRANDA. You needn't say that it makes you happy, Juan, but it will make *me* happy, if I see, someday, that *you* are happy. [THE SERVANT *comes in with a silver tray; he serves them, goes out.*]

DON JUAN. Would you pass the bread, please?

MIRANDA. Certainly.

They begin to eat, slowly, in silence. Very slowly . . .
The curtain falls.

THE GREAT RAGE OF PHILIP HOTZ

(*Die Grosse Wut des Philipp Hotz*)

A play in one act

*First performed March 29, 1958, at the
Schauspielhaus, Zurich.*

CHARACTERS

PHILIP HOTZ, *man of letters*
DODO, *his wife*
WILFRID, *a friend*
CLARISSA, *his wife*
A Young Furniture Mover
An Old Furniture Mover
An Elderly Lady
A Customs Officer
A Waiter
Two Legionnaires

The action takes place in a room of a modern apartment.

A Note Concerning the Setting

I imagine a room of approximately twelve by eighteen feet
and having the aspect of a podium, without walls, and some-
what elevated above the stage level. The limits of this
room—the playing area, properly speaking—are indicated by
this slight elevation, so that walls are not necessary; it is a
scene within the scene, a springboard, a lecture platform.
Naturally, the danger that is always possible in naturalism
is not sufficiently avoided if the principal actor does not
sufficiently play the "clown." The scene within the scene
—the podium slightly narrower at the front, an ancient,
rather rustic wardrobe at the rear, empty space on three sides
of the podium—gives the principal actor the freedom to
enter the scene or to leave it at will, disregarding the invisible
"walls" and without the other actors taking any note of this.
And this passage back and forth between play and direct address to the audience should always be completely visible.

M. F.

THE GREAT RAGE OF PHILIP HOTZ

The room is empty. Enter HOTZ, *pale with rage, dressed in
an unbuttoned raincoat; he starts to fill a tiny valise.*

HOTZ. Just so you will know: I am now packing my suitcase.
Shirt, toothbrush, pajamas. As for the rest, I suppose it
will be furnished by the Foreign Legion. [*Feminine sobs
are heard emanating from the wardrobe.*] I'll finish up
here as quickly as possible. Calm yourself! As soon as
I'm finished, I'll let you out of the wardrobe. [*He closes
his suitcase.*] See—I'm finished with the suitcase already.
[*He sets the valise to one side.*] Now all that I have left
to do is the demolition of the apartment. [*He looks about,
as if wondering where to start, tears down a curtain,
crumples it up, and then, as if awakened by the sight of
the crumpled curtain, he comes down toward the footlights and addresses the audience.*] I know. You too, ladies
and gentlemen, are completely in sympathy with my wife.
But, please . . . one moment. You too, I know, you too
are of the opinion that marriage is possible. [*He takes a
cigarette.*] I have no intention of getting overheated. Not
the slightest. . . . [*He smokes.*] Now, I don't know,
ladies and gentlemen, what Dodo has told you. . . .
[*Telephone rings.*] Excuse me. [*He picks up the phone and
answers.*] One moment, please. [*He puts the receiver aside
and comes back to speak to the audience.*] If you too,
ladies and gentlemen, like all those who have never been
married to Dodo, like our justice of the peace—if you too
feel that we should give it another try, two sensible persons like ourselves, or—as our justice of the peace chooses
to express it—sleep on it overnight . . . [*He remembers
that he has left the telephone off the hook.*] One moment,
please. [*Into the telephone again.*] Hello! Yes, this is Mr.

77

Hotz. No, I am not my wife, I am sorry to say. I will give
her the message. [*He hangs up and speaks toward the
wardrobe.*] That was your lawyer. You're to call him up
as soon as you come in. [*He comes back to the footlights.*]
Well, what I said was: I will demolish the entire apartment—which Dodo flatly refused to believe me capable
of—and then I will go off and join the Foreign Legion.
. . . [*Doorbell rings.*] Ah, here are my furniture movers!

*He goes back into the "room" and then exits through the
door. Sobs from within the wardrobe. A rather intimidated-
looking* ELDERLY LADY *enters and remains standing just inside the room, while* HOTZ *returns to the footlights from the
side.*

Hotz. I said: I will demolish the whole apartment—but,
naturally, she refused to take me seriously; she smiled; she
imagined we would come back home arm in arm; she
didn't think I was capable of such a thing—and why?
Simply because I am a cultivated man. [*He takes out
another cigarette, discovers he already has one lit, and
finally stamps out the lit one on the floor.*] Well, we shall
see what we shall see. [*He returns to the "room."*] I beg
your pardon.

THE ELDERLY LADY. Er—I trust I am not intruding . . . ?

Hotz. Not at all. [*He offers her a chair, and she sits down.*]
Now then, what has my wife told you?

THE ELDERLY LADY. To come when her husband would be
at home.

Hotz. Let's speak freely! [*He lights the new cigarette.*] I
do not dispute that Dodo is a person of great merit. And
I do not need a justice of the peace, nor an Aunt Bertha,
to remind me that my wife is altogether too good for
me. . . .

THE ELDERLY LADY. But, sir . . .

Hotz. Please. Let me finish. [*He takes up a stance as though
preparing for a debate.*] What do you understand, madam,
by the term "marriage"? [THE ELDERLY LADY *begins to
search in her handbag.*] Madam, I have taken the trouble
to ascertain the mean average ratio of adulteries within
the circle of my friends and acquaintances—and it would
certainly not be less on the lower levels of society— further-
more, I have counted only those absolutely incontestable

cases, which can be verified by at least three disinterested persons. And what is the result? I have arrived—including men up to fifty years of age, mind you—I have arrived at a figure in the neighborhood of 5.1067. Please! Premeditated adulteries entered into with care by knowing men of the world and brought to light only by accident, so to speak, or minor flirtations, which can, to be sure, sometimes go further and even surpass in ardor full-scale adulteries—all these I leave out of account, and still my mean average ratio of adulteries per man remains: 5.1067. And despite this, madam, these persons (I name no names) will continue to insist that marriage is possible.

THE ELDERLY LADY. But, sir . . .

HOTZ. Aunt Bertha! [*He forces himself to be calm.*] I have taken all the steps for a divorce in peace and in friendship. Everything, according to propriety and custom: Madame Simone Dorothy Hotz, nee Haussmann, files suit against her husband on the charge of adultery—this takes account of everything that is necessary, notice. My counterdeposition, in order to spare Dodo, is based solely on incompatibility—which, by the bye, is no exaggeration; I have never, as she herself will be the first to tell you, understood my wife—and never less than this morning when Dodo, this woman—I say "woman," and I am being polite—quite simply and without warning withdrew her suit for divorce. [THE ELDERLY LADY *stands up.*] Sit down! [THE ELDERLY LADY *sits down.*] My most beloved and esteemed Aunt Bertha . . .

THE ELDERLY LADY. You are making a mistake, sir, a serious mistake!

HOTZ. Unfortunately, Aunt Bertha, I am *not* making a mistake. It is not these infidelities which are ruining our household—they would be enough, I admit, and they are, in a way, repugnant—but no, it is the fact, my dear woman, the simple yet enormous fact that I am a man and an intellectual and my wife is a woman. [*The doorbell rings.*] And that, my dear Aunt Bertha, will not change, nor will it change anything, if, as our justice of the peace suggests, we sleep on it overnight. [*The doorbell rings.*] Quite the contrary, in fact. [*The doorbell rings.*] Excuse me? [*He goes out.*]

THE ELDERLY LADY. Madam? Madam? [*She cocks her head, listening, trying to discover the source of the sobs.*]

In the meantime, HOTZ *reappears by the wings, carrying a saw in his hand.*

HOTZ. Oh, no, ladies! No, no! It's not jealousy. Please don't imagine that I am jealous because Dodo has been carrying on for a long time with this dirty dog of . . . a director of a factory for making machines for exportation. . . . Oh, no! By no means! [Two FURNITURE MOVERS, *equipped with straps, enter the room.*] I'll be right there! [*Back to the public; he leans against the proscenium arch.*] I am not an Eskimo, ladies, an Eskimo who considers his wife as his property. To my way of thinking, there are no property rights in love. I can not be jealous, ladies, as a matter of principle; I simply can't be. [*The saw in his hand begins to tremble more and more as he grows angrier.*] But when a woman who has scarcely arrived in the courtroom suddenly withdraws her suit for divorce . . . well, I ask you . . . ! What about the settlements? And fidelity— yes, fidelity in all the circumstances of life? And . . . and solidarity between husband and wife? What becomes of all these, eh? I ask you: what the devil do you make of a marriage then? [*He goes back to the "room," but then returns to the footlights once more.*] She won't take me seriously; that's what it comes to; she simply won't take me seriously! [*He goes back into the "room."*] Gentlemen, you won't need these straps.

THE OLD FURNITURE MOVER. Oh? Why not?

HOTZ. I am—er—liquidating everything. [THE ELDERLY LADY *stands up.*] To put it in a nutshell, Aunt Bertha, I'm sorry, but I . . . [*She hands him a prospectus.*] What's this?

THE ELDERLY LADY. It's for the demonstration, sir.

HOTZ. You mean you're not Aunt Bertha? [*He addresses* THE FURNITURE MOVERS.] You have a crowbar? And the pliers —I particularly specified pliers, and a handsaw, and a crowbar. What about pliers?

THE YOUNG FURNITURE MOVER. We've got them.

HOTZ. And the handsaw?

THE YOUNG FURNITURE MOVER. You've got it.

HOTZ [*sees that he is still carrying the saw*]. Ah. Good! [*He gives the prospectus back to* THE ELDERLY LADY.] I'm sorry, madam, but I don't need a vacuum cleaner. . . . [*He accompanies her to the door.*] Now then—we haven't much time, gentlemen, let's get started! For example, the pictures. You take a kitchen knife, or whatever you happen to have in your hand, and you cut—from the upper left toward the bottom—thus. You see? [*He demonstrates on a picture on the back wall.*] Understand? [THE FURNITURE MOVERS *exchange glances.*] What's the matter?

THE YOUNG FURNITURE MOVER. You want to destroy . . . ?

HOTZ. Everything that isn't attached, right—such as the sanitary installations, the kitchen appliances, the radiators, the bathtub, the wiring, et cetera, et cetera. . . . There's an ash tray, young man.

THE YOUNG FURNITURE MOVER. What about it?

HOTZ. It's for ashes.

THE YOUNG FURNITURE MOVER [*tapping the ash off his cigarette*]. Okay.

HOTZ. The rug, you see, belongs to my wife's trousseau. [*He moves toward the writing desk.*] Dodo, where did you put the list of your trousseau? [THE FURNITURE MOVERS *start to pick up a large grandfather clock.*] I'll take charge of that clock personally; it's an old family souvenir. [THE FURNITURE MOVERS *put it down in the middle of the room.*] And as for all sorts of feminine apparatus around the place, such as dresses and lingerie, et cetera, magazines, lipstick, silk stockings, et cetera, brassieres, little bottles, combs, et cetera, letters from Argentina, slippers, et cetera, music books and girdles and fingernail scissors, et cetera, everything under the sun that grates on a man's nerves, in short . . . don't touch a thing, please. My wife is very—er—susceptible. And, as for the sawing, please do it outside, in the hallway. [THE FURNITURE MOVERS *are adjusting their straps to lift the wardrobe.*] Stop! For the love of God! The wardrobe stays. Good God! [THE FURNITURE MOVERS *put the wardrobe back down.*] Excuse me! [*He mops his brow.*] Here is the list of the trousseau.

THE FURNITURE MOVERS *pick up the table and chairs.*

THE YOUNG FURNITURE MOVER. And what do you want done with these?

HOTZ. Cut off the legs.

THE YOUNG FURNITURE MOVER. Cut them . . . ? How short?

HOTZ. Oh . . . fairly . . .

THE YOUNG FURNITURE MOVER [*indicating with his finger*]. About here?

HOTZ. It's up to you, really. [THE FURNITURE MOVERS *go out, carrying the chairs and table.* HOTZ *goes over and knocks at the wardrobe.*] Dodo? [*He places his ear against the wardrobe door.*] Why are you holding your breath? [*Sawing is heard offstage.*] You hear, Dodo? I've hired a couple of furniture movers—in order to speed things up. So be calm. [*A piece of wood is heard to fall; the sound of sawing stops.*] The first leg . . . [*The sawing noise starts again.*] Now, it's simply a question of not getting all up in the air! [*A piece of wood is heard to fall.*] The second leg! [*He covers his face with his hand just as a third piece of wood is heard to fall.*] The third leg! [*He goes over and kicks the clock, which chimes deeply.*] Now, it's just a matter of keeping calm. [*He starts to look for something, while the sound of sawing recommences.*] Dodo, where did you put the screwdriver? [*He looks toward the wardrobe.*] Dodo! Are you crazy? [*A tiny wisp of smoke rises from the wardrobe.*] I decline all responsibility, you hear? I shut you in that wardrobe, yes, but you are an adult, Dodo, and you know how dangerous it is to smoke in a wardrobe full of clothes! [*A wisp of smoke rises from the wardrobe.*] You hear me? [*A puff of smoke rolls up from the wardrobe.* HOTZ *moves toward the footlights; to the audience.*] There you are, ladies and gentlemen, you see? You can confirm it yourselves. She simply counts on my bad conscience. . . . [*He goes back to the "room."*] Just so you will know, Dodo— [*He takes his suitcase.*]—since you can't see me: here I am, my suitcase in my hand, whether you believe it or not. . . .

THE OLD FURNITURE MOVER [*entering*]. How do you want the curtains, sir?

HOTZ. The curtains?

THE OLD FURNITURE MOVER. Cut up in pieces or burned?

Hotz. In pieces, I think.

The Old Furniture Mover. In ribbons, or . . . ?

Hotz. In ribbons, please, yes.

The Old Furniture Mover. How wide?

Hotz. The width of my hand, let's say.

The Old Furniture Mover. Four inches?

Hotz. Approximately. [The Old Furniture Mover *takes a small ruler out of his pocket.*] Give or take an inch. But I really don't care; you can cut them into triangles if you like. Whatever amuses you, my friend, whatever amuses you! [The Old Furniture Mover *takes the curtain and goes.*] Okay, Dodo. Now I'm going. . . . I don't see why it should always be me who tries to patch things up with us. . . . Dodo, I'm going now . . . [*A wisp of smoke comes out of the wardrobe.* Hotz *puts his suitcase down and comes downstage again to address the audience.*] It's my wife who is driving me to the Foreign Legion, you see? Simply because she won't take me seriously: she doesn't believe I am capable of leaving. [*He takes a timetable from his pocket.*] Geneva, Lyons, Marseilles. [*He riffles through it.*] I know what they say about the Foreign Legion—and so does Dodo, oh, yes! [*He puts the timetable back in his pocket.*] 5:23 P.M. Connection: 10:07 P.M. [*He goes back to the "room." He picks up his suitcase.*] For the last time, Dodo: here it is. I'm all ready. [*He knocks at the wardrobe.*] Dodo? [*Sawing is heard in the distance.*] I gave them the list. The things in your trousseau. I've told them to touch nothing in your trousseau, not a thing. I am leaving with one shirt, one toothbrush, and one pair of pajamas, as you can see; I don't have your volume of Corneille. . . . Well, you'll be able to earn your living, I have no doubt of that. . . . Say good-bye to your family for me. . . . Oh, yes, they'll say, he's chosen the path of least resistance, he's gone off to the Legion. . . . Well, we're never going to see each other again. . . . Er—if any mail comes for me in the next few years . . .

The Young Furniture Mover *enters, carrying the armchair with its legs sawed off. The seat of the chair is now about four or five inches above the floor.*

The Young Furniture Mover. There's someone out in the vestibule, sir.

HOTZ. I don't want to see anyone.

THE YOUNG FURNITURE MOVER. He wants to talk with madam.

A wisp of smoke rises from the wardrobe.

HOTZ. I decline all responsibility!

He goes out. THE YOUNG FURNITURE MOVER, *curious, turns the key which is in the lock of the wardrobe and opens it.* DODO *steps out. She is tiny, delightfully pretty (despite her tears), smoking a cigarette.*

DODO. Is there still an ash tray in the place? [THE YOUNG FURNITURE MOVER *hands her an ash tray. She puts out her cigarette, goes to the telephone, and dials a number.*] Hotz. Yes—Mrs. Hotz. Might I talk to my lawyer? [*To* THE YOUNG FURNITURE MOVER.] Thank you. [*Into the telephone.*] Hello! Yes! What? But I've been trying for three hours . . . what? What's that? But I tell you, he's doing it; it's no longer a matter of words, he's doing it! What? What did you say? No, I didn't say a word. But what could I do? He shut me in the wardrobe! [*To* THE YOUNG FURNITURE MOVER.] You're my witness. [*She hangs up.*] Even my own lawyer won't believe me.

Men's voices are heard offstage. DODO *runs over and hides behind a curtain as* HOTZ, *still with his raincoat on and with a screwdriver in his hand, enters, ushering in a guest who is rubbing his hands together cheerfully.*

WILFRID. Who would have believed it, Philip, who would have believed it? I have scarcely arrived, my plane has barely landed, and here I am! I'm still a little giddy. . . . Three years in Argentina, old boy, three years in that climate, you can't imagine it, three years, mind you, three years of nothing to do but make money! No, you can't imagine it. . . . [*He looks around.*] Nothing changed, nothing changed! [*An embarrassed silence.*] And you, Philip, are you still trying to be a writer? Ha Ha! [*He laughs and slaps* HOTZ *on the back.*] Philip, my friend!

HOTZ. Wilfrid . . .

WILFRID. No, dear boy, no, you can't imagine what it was like, three years down there, and now, scarcely am I back in Europe, and . . . ah, it's really like coming home!

HOTZ. Please . . . [*He offers him the cut-down chair.*] Please . . .

WILFRID *sits down, as though there were nothing wrong. He obviously does not wish to show any signs of embarrassment. Offstage, renewed sounds of sawing.* HOTZ *seats himself astride the grandfather clock and begins to dismantle it with the screwdriver while* WILFRID *lights a cigar.*

WILFRID. Tell me . . . how is Dodo? [*He puffs at his cigar.*] Is she still doing her ceramics?

HOTZ. Not at the moment, no.

WILFRID. Where is she, then?

HOTZ [*getting up and going to the door*]. Er . . . will you fellows take this wardrobe out of here now? [*To* WILFRID.] Excuse me a moment. [*To* THE FURNITURE MOVERS, *who enter.*] Don't turn it over, please. [THE FURNITURE MOVERS *prepare their straps.*] Wilfrid, what can I offer you? I'm afraid we don't have any more glasses, though. Gin? Campari? Whisky? [THE FURNITURE MOVERS *tilt the wardrobe.*] Stop! You're out of your minds! Stop it! I expressly warned you: don't turn it over . . . !

THE OLD FURNITURE MOVER. But what if the door is too narrow?

HOTZ. Well, then . . . here . . . here, out on the balcony. [*He opens the door to the balcony. To* WILFRID.] Excuse me, Wilfrid . . .

HOTZ *mops his brow.* THE FURNITURE MOVERS *carry the wardrobe out onto the balcony.*

WILFRID. If you're so warm, why don't you take off your coat?

HOTZ *has locked the wardrobe door with the key, which is still in the keyhole; now he puts the key in his pocket.*

HOTZ. Thank God!

THE FURNITURE MOVERS *are gone, dragging their straps; meanwhile* HOTZ *seats himself astride the clock again and begins to take it apart with the screwdriver.* WILFRID *smokes his cigar.*

WILFRID. I asked you about Dodo. . . . [HOTZ *removes the face of the clock and throws it to one side.*] You tell me if I'm bothering you, will you, Philip?

HOTZ. No, no, not at all.

WILFRID. Word of honor?

HOTZ. Here, you can hold the screws. [*Puts them in his hand.*] And now, you can answer my question. . . . [*He tears off the door of the clock and throws it aside.*] Do you believe that such a thing as marriage is possible?

WILFRID. Which marriage?

HOTZ. Any one. Marriage in general.

At this moment, a spring flies out of the clock with a loud "boing!"

WILFRID. Did you hurt yourself? [HOTZ *sucks his finger.*] Tell me—just as a matter of curiosity—what are you doing there?

HOTZ. I'm taking an old clock apart.

WILFRID. Why?

HOTZ. Because I have no sense of humor.

WILFRID. Philip!

HOTZ. You feel that I have a sense of humor?

WILFRID. No.

HOTZ. Well, then . . . !

WILFRID. Who told you this?

HOTZ. Dodo, my wife, with whom you are acquainted, I believe. . . . She says: Number one, I am not a man; I talk, talk, talk; that's all that I know how to do. As contrasted, for example, with you. Her lawyer goes even further, but then that's what he's paid for—by me, naturally; he says: Your husband is schizoid. And then, number two: I have no sense of humor. As contrasted, for example, with you. [WILFRID *smiles.*] It is so pleasant of you, Wilfrid, to be able to smile in spite of everything. [THE OLD FURNITURE MOVER *brings in the table with the sawed-off legs.*] Thank you.

THE OLD FURNITURE MOVER. Now what?

HOTZ. The cellar. All the bottles are to be uncorked. On second thought, I'll do that myself. Just bring the bottles here.

THE OLD FURNITURE MOVER *goes out.*

WILFRID. Very interesting! [*He passes his hand over the cut-down table.*] Very interesting!

HOTZ. You think so?

WILFRID. Maybe you have no sense of humor, but when it comes to ideas—Philip, you've got them. [HOTZ *sucks his finger*.] Did you ever live in Japan? [HOTZ, *still sucking his finger, shakes his head*.] This is—er—your own idea? [HOTZ *nods his head, still sucking at his injured finger*.] Three years in Argentina, no, you can't imagine it, the lack of everything that is important to us, taste, culture, and . . . er . . . the whole . . . er . . . atmosphere. . . . [*He passes his hand over the cut-down table*.]

HOTZ. To return to our question. . . . [*He gives him another screw to hold*.] Are you really in love with her?

WILFRID. Who? My wife?

HOTZ. No. Mine. [WILFRID *starts violently*.] Don't drop my screws.

A great noise is heard offstage. THE YOUNG FURNITURE
MOVER *enters.*

THE YOUNG FURNITURE MOVER. Sorry. There was no other way to do it.

HOTZ. What was it?

THE YOUNG FURNITURE MOVER. The bed springs.

HOTZ. Ah. [THE YOUNG FURNITURE MOVER *goes*.] To return to our question . . .

WILFRID. Now wait just a minute! That's enough, now . . .

HOTZ. You feel, then, that marriage is possible?

WILFRID. If I didn't, I would . . . I would throw your screws through that window! [*He gets up abruptly*.] Absolutely!

HOTZ [*continues to busy himself with the screwdriver*]. I've always envied you your sense of humor, Wilfrid. Now is not the moment to lose it simply because you feel that I will not be amused by the knowledge that you have slept with my wife.

WILFRID. Philip!

HOTZ. Look, are you going to hold my screws for me or aren't you? [WILFRID *turns his back on* HOTZ.] I don't understand your indignation. . . . [THE OLD FURNITURE MOVER *enters and throws some pieces of wood down on the floor*.] What's this?

THE OLD FURNITURE MOVER. The bed slats.

HOTZ. Thank you. [THE OLD FURNITURE MOVER *goes out.*] To return to our question. . . [*Telephone bell.*] Excuse me. [*He answers.*] Hotz here. Yes, it's me. [*He sets down the receiver.*] Give me the screws! [*He takes the screws from* WILFRID, *throws them through the window, and picks up the receiver again.*] Are you still there? What? What's that? [*Covers the receiver and speaks to* WILFRED.] Are we making too much noise, would you say? [*He listens again a moment.*] Yes. Yes. Well, it was a rather large grandfather clock that fell over, yes. I own only one grandfather clock, Mrs. Oppikofer; they don't reproduce like rabbits. What? What's that? [*He holds the receiver with his shoulder, reaches in his pocket, and takes out a key.*] Here's the key.

WILFRID. The key?

HOTZ. You came to see Dodo. Take it! She is in the wardrobe out on the balcony.

WILFRID. Dodo?

HOTZ. Outside, on the balcony, yes. [*He offers him the key, but* WILFRID *doesn't take it.*] Mrs. Oppikofer, I will answer as soon as you stop shouting. [*He covers the receiver with his hand.*] By the way, how is your darling Clarissa? [*To telephone.*] My dear Mrs. Oppikofer, may I offer you the same? I assure you, it is I who am saying farewell to you. I'll be right down. [*He hangs up.*] I've never wound up so many thoroughly disagreeable affairs in one single day! I can hardly believe it myself. I've never been a man of action before. [*He takes out a comb and passes it through his hair.*] But the main thing now is to remain calm. . . .

THE OLD FURNITURE MOVER *enters with a large vase, which he unwraps; he speaks to* WILFRID.

THE OLD FURNITURE MOVER. Is this part of the trousseau?

WILFRED. *That* . . . ? Good heavens, what are you doing, handling it like that . . . ? That's a genuine Inca vase. . . .

THE OLD FURNITURE MOVER. Inca? What's that?

WILFRID. None of your business.

THE OLD FURNITURE MOVER. A gift for madam . . . ?

WILFRID. Well . . . er . . . yes . . .

THE OLD FURNITURE MOVER. Better speak up, sir, or it's
    kersmash for this one!

WILFRID. It was a gift from me to madam, yes. We've known
    each other since childhood, you understand. . . .

THE OLD FURNITURE MOVER. Okay. Trousseau.

He picks up the vase again and goes out. HOTZ *has been
combing his hair in preparation for his call on* MRS. OPPI-
KOFER. *Now he blows on his comb.*

HOTZ. To keep calm, that's the important thing . . . very
    calm. . . .

He puts the comb back in his pocket and goes out. WILFRID
*tiptoes over and casts a nervous glance toward the wardrobe,
which is outside on the balcony. Behind his back,* DODO *slips
out of her hiding place.*

DODO. Thank you, Wilfrid.

WILFRID. Dodo!

DODO. For the beautiful vase. [*He takes her by the shoulders,
    without a word.*] Give me a cigarette. [*He hands her a
    cigarette.*]

WILFRID. Dodo, he knows everything.

DODO. I know.

WILFRID. Who could have told him?

DODO. Me. [*He stands stunned into immobility; she reaches
    out and takes the cigarette lighter from him.*] And you—
    how are you?

HOTZ [*coming out by the wings and speaking to the audi-
    ence*]. Now, ladies and gentlemen, you are going to hear
    what I cannot hear myself—I am downstairs in Mrs. Op-
    pikofer's apartment, don't forget—but I can imagine it.
    [*He remains near the footlights, looking out at the audi-
    ence.*]

DODO. He is primitive.

HOTZ. She means me, of course.

DODO. He is egocentric.

HOTZ. It's still me she's talking about.

DODO. He thinks of no one but himself.

HOTZ. And now . . . the analysis——

DODO. He is schizophrenic——

HOTZ. Schizoid.

Dodo. —or something like that.

                    Hotz *takes out a cigarette*.

Hotz. And then?

Dodo. Marriage understood as a sort of spiritual union!

Hotz. Precisely!

Dodo. And all the rest with all those other women! *That's* what he really wants! Liberty within marriage! And for me to be free to do whatever I want to.

Hotz. My wife is not my property.

Dodo. He doesn't know what jealousy is! Talk about your hypocrites! And it's all a matter of principle! Don't talk to *me* about hypocrisy! He reproaches me with nothing, nothing. . . . [Hotz *calmly lights his cigarette*.] What kind of a marriage is that? [Hotz *smokes*.]

Hotz. It's hopeless. For seven years now I've explained to her what I understand by marriage, or, according to my wife, I have argued with her in attempting to explain to her that, for me, marriage is not possible except as a sort of spiritual union, a union with liberty, equality, and sincerity. [Dodo *smiles*.] A kind of spiritual enterprise. [Dodo *smiles*.] Marriages are not made in bed. [Dodo *smiles*.] I say . . .

Dodo. If you could only hear him talk . . .

Hotz. A marriage that is not based on conjugal fidelity . . .

Dodo. I know it all by heart . . .

Hotz. A marriage that does not eventually come to the realization that . . .

Dodo. What a hypocrite! [*She screams*.] And oh, is he jealous!

Hotz [*shouts*]. That's a lie!

Dodo. He simply wants to lord it over me. That's all. For, as far as I am concerned, you see, he thinks I don't have the *right* to be jealous . . . !

Hotz [*smoking*]. You do not have the right to be jealous.

Dodo. Oh—it's . . . it's ignoble the way he wants to lord it over me!

Hotz. No one has the right to be jealous. [*He smokes*.]

Dodo. It will have been exactly a year tomorrow that I first told him . . . about us. And it was not until today that he finally got around to showing some anger. Him and his introversion! Today—at last! [THE YOUNG FURNITURE

Mover *comes in and empties a wastebasket full of trash on the floor.*] What's that?

WILFRID. Trash, I believe.

DODO. Simply because I said to him: You will never do it. I know you, Philip! [THE OLD FURNITURE MOVER *empties a wastebaket full of trash.*]

WILFRID. And what does that mean?

DODO. Simply so that I'll take him seriously the next time he gets angry and starts pretending that our marriage is impossible . . . ! [*She shakes her head.*] And the curtains! The furniture! The pictures! I've never heard of such a thing! Just because the justice of the peace called him a cultivated man! [*She takes a cigarette.*]

HOTZ. She's beginning to get the idea. [*He goes back up onto the platform to light her cigarette for her.*]

WILFRID. Look here, even those lovely drinking glasses I gave you are being thrown out!

DODO *puffs at her cigarette, and* HOTZ *comes back down to the footlights.*

DODO. And still—with everything—I love him! [HOTZ, *standing near the footlights, continues to smoke, gazing out at the audience.* Despite which I can't go running to the railroad station and pull him off the train every time he threatens me with his damned Foreign Legion! Can I? Simply to prove to him that I take him seriously! [*She starts to cry again.*]

WILFRID. Why did he lock you in the wardrobe?

HOTZ. She knows perfectly well why.

WILFRID. Why?

HOTZ. Go on, tell him!

DODO. Simply because—as I told you—simply because I said to him: You won't do it, Philip—I know you! [*She starts to cry again.*]

HOTZ. Please note that my friend, Wilfrid, no longer dreams of touching my wife now that he has perceived that we are in the process of getting a divorce.

DODO [*sobbing*]. S-simply . . . because I said to him: Y-you w-won't do it, Ph-philip. . . . I know you . . . you've been saying that for seven years now! [HOTZ *goes back into the scene to offer her an ash tray.*] And, despite everything, I've been so happily married! [*She puts her cigarette in the ash tray;* Hotz *comes back down front again.*] Why should I want to get a divorce?

WILFRID [*puts his arm around* DODO's *shoulders*]. Oh! Dodo . . . !

DODO. Oh! Wilfrid . . . !

HOTZ. Oh oh! Ah, well, even so . . .

WILFRID. You love him?

HOTZ. Oh, yes, never fear. [WILFRID *strokes her hair.*] Never fear. [*He takes out another cigarette, even though he still has one lit.*] Ladies and gentlemen, it is possible that you find me egocentric when I imagine that they are talking about me all the time. But it's true! For them, I am the sole subject of conversation which never grows tedious . . . [*He lights his new cigarette.*]

WILFRID. And you think that he loves you too?

HOTZ. She thinks so.

DODO. Why does he always want to assert himself? Why does he always say he wants to take the blame for the infidelities in our marrage? To make me play the part of the madonna. And why? Simply because at the trial there was not a word mentioned of that insane jealousy of his which sends the blood rushing to his head every time he thinks of it—not once did his attorney mention how jealous Philip is, oh, no! No, he prefers to take all the blame upon himself and to pay through the nose like an adulterous husband, to ruin himself up to the time I am sixty years of age—anything to assert himself, you notice, and to make *me* feel guilty! [*Tapping her foot.*] To make *me* feel guilty—well, he won't do it! [*She raises her voice.*] I will not grant him a divorce, and I *will* remain his wife—to the end of my days—until he gives in, until he absolutely gives in!

HOTZ. What? [*Shouts.*] What?

DODO [*calming herself*]. He doesn't betray himself by the flicker of an eyelash; he never shouts, but within—within, he's a caveman!

HOTZ [*shouting more loudly than ever*]. What do you know about it?

DODO [*moving toward* WILFRID]. Oh! Wilfrid . . .

WILFRID. Oh! Dodo . . . [*They embrace.*]

HOTZ. At last. [*He is very ill at ease, nevertheless.*] As I've already said: In reality, I couldn't possibly know what has been going on here. . . . In reality, of course, I am at this moment downstairs in Mrs. Oppikofer's apartment. [*He crushes out his cigarette.*] Ladies and gentlemen, don't look! I'm not going to look at them any more. We can imagine it just as well. And if you ever find yourselves in my situation, gentlemen, I advise you . . . [*He turns and sneaks a look at them in spite of himself.*] Turtledoves!

A *terrible detonation is heard offstage, a sort of jangling musical discord.*

WILFRID. What was that?

DODO. I have no idea.

WILFRID. Now, look here, my good men, if this uproar doesn't cease immediately, but immediately . . . ! [*Another crash.*] What the devil are they doing with the grand piano? [*A series of crashing chords.*]

HOTZ. Division of property. [DODO *begins to cry.*] "If the division of property occurs in the course of a marriage, the conjugal property is to be divided into two parts: one part, the personal property of the husband; the other part, the personal property of the wife." [*Another crash.*] Conjugal Law, Chapter One, Article 189. [*He fastens his collar button.*] I remind you once again, ladies and gentlemen, at this moment I am downstairs with Mrs. Oppikofer, the landlady. [*He exits at the wings.*]

WILFRID. Why did you tell him?

DODO. But he told *me* first.

WILFRID. What?

DODO. About his affair with Clarissa.

WILFRID. Clarissa?!

DODO. Sincerity, pure and simple! I'm capable of it, too— it's as simple as that. All aboard for marriage based on sincerity!

WILFRID. What has Philip done with my wife?

DODO. The same thing you've done with me . . . [*She dries her eyes with his pocket handkerchief.*] You didn't know about that?

HOTZ *comes out at the wings, a paper in his hands.*

HOTZ [*to the audience*]. There! Our lease is now broken. [*He tears up the paper.*]

WILFRID. Clarissa?

DODO. Don't shout . . .

WILFRID. *My* Clarissa?!

DODO. Everyone in the place can hear you.

WILFRID. Women! Whores! [*He rushes out.*]

DODO. He's even more primitive than Philip. [*She follows him.*]

HOTZ. And now there's nothing left for me to do but to say my good-byes. [*He calls.*] Gentlemen! [THE FURNITURE MOVERS *come in; they are eating their lunch.*] Bring the wardrobe back in, will you? It's starting to rain cats and dogs. [*He remains down near the footlights.*] No, ladies and gentlemen, never fear—I am not schizoid. I admit: In thought I have been up here while I was in reality downstairs arranging about the lease. But I am just as sure of the details of this conversation I have imagined between my wife and my friend as I am—well, as I am that my wife is locked in that wardrobe! No, no, I am not schizoid! [*He goes back up into the "room."* THE FURNITURE MOVERS *bring the wardrobe back in.*] All right? All right? Is it coming? [*They nod, their mouths full.*] Is it heavy? [*They shake their heads, chewing, their mouths full.*] Ah, what muscles! What biceps! [*They put the wardrobe back where it was originally.*] Thank you, gentlemen, a thousand thanks. [THE FURNITURE MOVERS *go out, dragging their straps;* HOTZ *addresses the wardrobe even before they have left.*] Dodo, have you gotten wet? [*He knocks on the wardrobe.*] Dodo? [*He picks up his suitcase.*] Dodo, I'm leaving now—for the Foreign Legion. [*He puts his ear against the wardrobe door.*] Why are you still holding your breath? [*He hesitates, uncertain.*] It's undignified, Dodo—the way you treat me. For seven years now, every time you're really up against it, you hold your breath—just because you think you can scare me to death and make me think I've killed you. Dodo, that's no way to have a good marriage. You count on the fact that I love you and you think you can do whatever you want to with me—simply because you're the weaker of the two. [*He picks up his suitcase again.*] This time, I'm really going. You see? [*He glances at his watch.*] I'm catching the train for

Geneva at 5:23, with a connection for Marseilles at 10:07. You're silent now—but just in case you should change your mind later today, you can reach me in care of General Delivery, Marseilles. [*At this moment we begin to hear, distantly and rather faintly, the sound of all the church bells in the town.*] Good-bye!

THE YOUNG FURNITURE MOVER *comes in.*

THE YOUNG FURNITURE MOVER. Sir! [HOTZ *starts.*] About the radio. Just a bit of advice—if I were you, I wouldn't sell it at any price. That's a terrific set you've got there. I know a little something about radios. The amplifier alone is worth plenty. But what I wanted to know was: Wouldn't it be all right if we demolished it sort of carefully—so it could be put back together again?

HOTZ. If you want to, fine.

THE YOUNG FURNITURE MOVER. You see, I'm getting married pretty soon, and . . .

HOTZ. Whatever you want to do with it . . . [THE YOUNG FURNITURE MOVER *exits.*] Good-bye. I said: Good-bye. [*The sound of church bells is augmented by the sound of a new and nearer one.*] It will be Easter tomorrow . . . remember our Easter in Rome, Dodo? Just a year ago . . . nevertheless, I'm still leaving! [*He embraces the wardrobe.*] I hope you'll be very happy, Dodo. [DODO *enters with her arms full of paper bags.*] Dodo!?

DODO. Yes?

HOTZ. No!

DODO. What's the matter?

HOTZ [*stares at her, thunderstruck, and puts his hand in his pocket*]. Just a minute, just a minute . . . [*He takes the key out of his pocket and opens the wardrobe.*] Dodo? . . . Dodo? . . . Dodo? [*He starts to throw all the clothes out of the wardrobe until it is quite empty, then climbs into it himself.*] I don't want to see you any more!

THE OLD FURNITURE MOVER *comes in carrying a violin.*

THE OLD FURNITURE MOVER. Excuse me, sir, but we've got to finish up. I just wanted to know if this is part of the trousseau also.

HOTZ. My violin?

THE OLD FURNITURE MOVER. On the list I have: "One old violin, Italian, with accessories, late eighteenth century, gift from Aunt Bertha"—and then it's crossed out.

HOTZ. Crossed out?

THE OLD FURNITURE MOVER. What does that mean?

DODO. It means you paid her for it, Philip—remember?

THE OLD FURNITURE MOVER. That's all I needed to know. [HOTZ *stares at him, still stunned*.] The violin does not belong to madam?

HOTZ. No.

THE OLD FURNITURE MOVER. That's all I needed to know. Good. [*He breaks the violin across his knee and goes out*.]

HOTZ. I don't want to see you any more. [*He exits*.]

DODO. Where are you going? [*She seats herself on the cut-down table and begins to take food out of the paper bags*.] I've got half a pizza. Do you want some of it?

HOTZ *comes out at the wings, down to the footlights, and addresses the audience*.

HOTZ. Now look. I've forgotten my suitcase. [*He rubs his chin*.]

DODO [*sitting on the table and talking as though* HOTZ *were just outside the door*]. Philip—you want sausage or cheese? [*She is starting to make sandwiches*.]

HOTZ [*to the audience*]. I simply can't get it through my head that she's not in that wardrobe. . . . I had the key in my pocket; the wardrobe was locked. . . . I understand it all less and less the more I think about it. . . . [*He takes out a cigarette*.] Well—one last cigarette! [*He lights it*.] And then I've got to go back and get that damned suitcase.

DODO. Your sandwich is ready! [*She calls sweetly*.] Philip! [*She turns around and sees* THE TWO FURNITURE MOVERS.]

THE YOUNG FURNITURE MOVER. We're all through, ma'am.

DODO. Oh. Well, if you want a tip, my husband is just outside there, in the vestibule.

THE OLD FURNITURE MOVER. No, ma'am, he's not.

DODO. Oh? Well, then, he must be on the stairway.

THE OLD FURNITURE MOVER. And if he's not there either?

DODO. All right, then, he must be in the Café Algiers, next door! [THE FURNITURE MOVERS *put their caps on*.] Happy

Easter! [THE FURNITURE MOVERS *go out wordlessly.*]
Philip . . . ?

HOTZ *comes up into the "room."*

HOTZ. All right—I'm going. [*He picks up his suitcase.*] Good
luck.

DODO [*looks at him*]. Do you know, I really can't stand you?

HOTZ. Dodo . . .

DODO. But there's one thing I'd like to know—really: Why
have you been wearing your raincoat ever since this morning? [*She starts to nibble at a sandwich.*]

HOTZ. Dodo, I'm going! [*He glances at his watch.*] Do you
have the right time?

DODO. 4:48.

HOTZ *resets his watch.*

HOTZ. Dodo, this is no way to have a good marriage; you do
whatever you want to do with me, just because you're the
weaker.

DODO. What are you talking about? What have I done?

HOTZ. I have to catch the train for Geneva: 5:23. Connection for Marseilles: 10:07. You're silent now, but just remember—if you should change your mind, my address is:
General Delivery, Marseilles.

DODO. I'm not being silent.

HOTZ. Well—I've got to get going. . . .

DODO. Where to?

HOTZ. Good luck!

Silence. The sound of bells outside.

DODO. And when will you be coming back?

Silence. Bells.

HOTZ. Tomorrow will be Easter. . . . Just a year ago,
Dodo—our Easter in Rome . . . all the same, I'm going!

DODO *starts to make a sandwich;* HOTZ *finally exits.*

DODO. I didn't buy any smoked salmon today; I thought
we'd better start economizing a little, Philip. This is going to turn out to be an expensive day for you. . . .

HOTZ [*comes out at the wings, suitcase in hand, and addresses the audience again*]. Now, if she's coming to call
me back—even though, in the early days of our marriage
she never came farther than the front door—if she *is*,

mind you, it's because she's finally coming to believe that I am *capable* of leaving—in which case, it's no longer necessary for me to leave. [*Glances at his watch.*] Let's hope her watch was right. [*He listens to his watch, then winds it.*]

DODO [*turns around; sees that nobody is there*]. Philip . . . I asked you if you wanted some of the pickled herring?

HOTZ. And what if they won't take me at Marseilles?

Doorbell.

DODO. Come in!

Enter CLARISSA, *taking off her gloves.*

CLARISSA. This is the last straw!

DODO. You?

CLARISSA. He struck me!

DODO. Who?

CLARISSA. Wilfrid—my husband!

DODO *puts the food to one side.*

DODO. Sit down.

CLARISSA *angrily throws her gloves aside.*

CLARISSA. What on earth got into you—I would really like to know—what on earth got into you to tell my husband that I've been having an affair with *your* husband?

DODO. Philip told me so.

CLARISSA. Philip?

DODO. Yes.

CLARISSA. Well, if that isn't the absolute last straw!

DODO *continues to eat.*

DODO. Oh, that's one of his great ideas, you know—absolute sincerity as the basis of a happy marriage.

CLARISSA *picks up her gloves again.*

CLARISSA. There has never been anything between us! [*She tosses one glove away again.*] Never! [*She throws the second glove.*] Never! [*She bursts into tears.*]

HOTZ [*to the audience*]. If Dodo now learns that I have never cheated on her—and if she believes it—she'll never believe me again! But I've really got to go! Really!

DODO. We women, we have no concept of solidarity. That's too bad. We went to the same school together, we two,

and at the first sign of maturity, what happens? We have
but one goal: to trap some man and, if possible, to double
cross our own sister. [*She offers* CLARISSA *a bite to eat.*]

CLARISSA. Thank you!

She and DODO *each take an apple.*

DODO. So—you have come all the way from Argentina to tell
me that this is untrue. Did you have a nice flight?

CLARISSA. Simone!

DODO. Now, please—no soap-opera!

CLARISSA. It's not true!

DODO *polishes her apple.*

DODO. I asked you if you had a nice flight. [*She bites into her
apple.*]

CLARISSA. What do I have to do to make you believe me,
Simone?

DODO. Nothing. [*She offers her the paper bag full of apples.*]
These apples aren't at all fattening.

CLARISSA. Oh? You think I'm too stout?

DODO. Let's get back to our business. [*Sitting and chewing
on her apple.*] And our business is—the man in the case.

CLARISSA. Yours or mine?

DODO. Mine. [CLARISSA *smiles.*] You understand, I will
never give him a divorce, and above all not for your sake!
Oh no! [*She shouts.*] Not for your sake!

HOTZ [*to the audience*]. You see? They're beginning to
shout already. [*He glances at his watch.*] This can't last
very long.

CLARISSA [*shouts*]. But it is simply and absolutely not true!
I'll shout it from the rooftops: It's not true! It's not true!
There has never been anything between us!

HOTZ [*to the audience*]. I'm going to miss my train. [*Looks
at his watch.*] Is that what people really think—that
there's never been anything between us? My God, is that
what they really think?

The two women—calm and dignified.

DODO. Oh? Are you leaving so soon?

CLARISSA. My dear, I do believe you're getting quite thin and
drawn-looking.

DODO. You haven't answered me.

CLARISSA. Quite, quite thin and drawn.

DODO. Philip is not your type, eh? [CLARISSA *shrugs*.] You don't know my husband very well.

CLARISSA. That's exactly what I've been trying to tell you.

DODO. You can libel my husband—and men in general—as much as you want to, but there's not a man in the world who would go around boasting of affairs that have never taken place—and in public, too!

CLARISSA. Your husband is a novelist.

DODO. What do you mean by that? [CLARISSA *rises*.] My husband is not a liar. [CLARISSA *touches up her make-up*.] Clarissa, I want to say something to you—— [*She seizes her*.] Between sisters, so to speak . . .

CLARISSA. Darling, I'd really rather not . . .

DODO. Very well. As you prefer. [*Releases her*.] But I'm still going to tell you something—— [CLARISSA *starts to put on her lipstick*.]

CLARISSA. Your Philip doesn't interest me. [*She passes her tongue across her painted lips*.]

DODO. Philip is the most bashful man in the world. Just between the two of us, he is bashful almost to the point of hypocrisy. But once he knows he has an audience, I can assure you—then he stops lying! Anything he says in public is true.

CLARISSA. Imagine that!

DODO. Yes, it's very strange.

CLARISSA. He doesn't lie. . . .

DODO. Never—not at any price. That's why I'm horrified by what Philip writes in his books: Just let him sense a public for his words and the most appalling flood of truths comes pouring out—for example, about our marriage— things that he couldn't bring himself to say in private for all the money in the world. [CLARISSA *picks up her gloves again*.]

CLARISSA. In short, you don't believe a word I'm saying. [DODO *picks up her apple again*.] Simone! [*She slips on her gloves*.] Nothing happened! I swear it! Absolutely nothing! [DODO *bites into her apple*.]

DODO. Thank you—I don't care to hear all the details.

HOTZ [*to the audience*]. This time, I'm really going! [*Takes

up his suitcase.] What am I waiting for? [*He checks to
be sure that this time he has his suitcase in his hand.*] I
have my suitcase this time.

CLARISSA. Happy Easter!

DODO is standing, eating her apple.

DODO. Happy Easter! [CLARISSA *goes.*] Have there ever been
two women who could believe each other when they were
talking about a man? [HOTZ *enters;* DODO *doesn't see
him.*] Happy Easter! [HOTZ *senses her mood and pops
back out again. She throws her apple furiously.*] That cow!

HOTZ [*comes out by the wings; to the audience*]. Sarcastic!
Now, that's something new for Dodo. She has been—I
don't know quite how to put it—but sarcastic . . . no,
this is quite new! [*He imitates her voice.*] "Happy Easter!"
[*He beams with hope.*] A different tone of voice! Yes,
that's something . . .

*He goes back up into the "room." DODO has seated herself
again on the cut-down table and is digging into one of the
paper bags.*

HOTZ. I'm going now.

She starts violently.

DODO. You?!

HOTZ places himself in front of her.

HOTZ. I'm going now.

She looks at him, stupefied. After a moment:

DODO. I—I'm so stupid. I forgot the tomatoes. [*She rum-
mages through the paper bags.*]

HOTZ. Well . . . I'll be going. [*He hesitates a moment,
then goes on out.*]

DODO. Oh—here they are! [*She takes out a tomato.*]

HOTZ [*comes out at the wings and addresses the audience
again*]. The trip to Geneva was terrible, every inch of the
way. So much so, that I was unable to remain angry—in
fact, I was forced to admit that the whole thing was idiotic, utterly idiotic!

NEWSPAPER VENDOR'S VOICE. Cigars, cigarettes, newspapers,
candy bars!

HOTZ. She was absolutely right, of course. I had no reason

to expect that Dodo would come running after me every
spring to pull me off of the train simply in order to make
me believe that she took me seriously . . .

NEWSPAPER VENDOR'S VOICE. Cigars, cigarettes, newspapers,
candy bars!

HOTZ. Obviously, it would be impossible for her to take me
seriously!

Sound of a train entering the station.

DODO [*on the telephone*]. Philip . . . ! Yes, yes, I'm at
home. Hello? I can't hear you. . . . You're in a phone
booth? Hello? Hello? Where are you? There's such a
racket. . . . Yes, yes, that's better. . . . How's everything in Geneva? Oh. Well . . .

*She hangs up slowly, stunned, while we hear the sounds of a
train starting and leaving the station; then she dials a
number.*

HOTZ [*to the audience*]. What else could I expect? I knew
perfectly well she'd be comfortably at home; she wasn't
even thinking about coming after me, the little
bitch . . . !

A SWISS CUSTOMS OFFICER *comes in.*

THE OFFICER. Swiss customs. [HOTZ *gives him his passport.*]

HOTZ. And to think that I still had some hopes in her!

THE OFFICER. Anything to declare?

HOTZ. What an imbecile I am!

THE OFFICER. Do you have anything to declare? [HOTZ
shows him his tiny suitcase.] Open it, please. [THE OF-
FICER *takes out the shirt, toothbrush, pajamas.*] Thank
you!

HOTZ. The only chance left for Dodo was that they might
make me undress here. That way, I could have missed my
connection. But now . . .

Meanwhile, THE OFFICER *has changed from a Swiss to a
French cap.*

THE OFFICER. Your passport, please. [HOTZ *nervously gives
him his passport.*]

HOTZ. But they're not even suspicious of me . . . [THE
OFFICER *returns the passport.*]

THE OFFICER. Anything to declare? [HOTZ *shows his*

suitcase.] Would you open it, please? [*He takes out the shirt, toothbrush, pajamas.*] Thank you and bon voyage, Monsieur.

HOTZ *puts his things back in the suitcase;* THE OFFICER *goes out.*

HOTZ [*miserably*]. They're all going to let me go.

DODO [*on the telephone*]. Operator, could you check and find out if that call really came from Geneva? . . . About five minutes ago, yes. . . . Thank you. [*She waits.*]

HOTZ [*to the audience*]. At Marseilles, the weather turned hot. . . . [*He takes off his jacket.*] First, I went to a small restaurant to have a cup of coffee—my favorite breakfast. . . .

Enter a WAITER; *he yawns.*

THE WAITER. Coffee?

HOTZ. With cream, please. [THE WAITER *yawns.*] Er—do you have sweet rolls? [THE WAITER *nods and exits.*] My favorite breakfast—coffee and rolls. [*He looks around.*] Naturally, not a sign of my wife—anywhere. [*The sound of military bugles.*] And now, in any case, it's too late.

While we hear bugles and drums playing a military march, an iron grillwork, like those fences that surround military camps, descends; it is gray in color, with a dirty tricolor on it; behind it, DODO *appears.*

DODO. Philip . . . ! Philip . . . !

Enter TWO DUSTY LEGIONNAIRES, *bayonets on their rifles, marching to the military music. Between them,* HOTZ, *his coat and jacket over his arm.* HOTZ *tries to stop to say something to* DODO, *but* THE LEGIONNAIRE *behind him nudges him with the bayonet to make him keep moving.* DODO *falls to her knees behind the grille and sobs bitterly.*

DODO. Philip . . . ! You're not cut out for the Foreign Legion . . . !

The military music fades, and the grille ascends out of sight once more. DODO *remains on her knees, sobbing, as* HOTZ *comes in slowly, dropping his coat and jacket.*

HOTZ. They didn't want me.

DODO. Philip!!

HOTZ. It's my myopia.

DODO [*throwing herself on his neck*]. Philip! [HOTZ *strokes her hair as she leans joyously against him.*]

HOTZ [*after a moment, to cover his embarrassment*]. Was there any mail for me—while I was gone?

Curtain.

WHEN THE WAR WAS OVER

(Als der Krieg zu Ende War)

A play in two acts

First performed January 8, 1949, at the Schauspielhaus, Zurich.

CHARACTERS

AGNES ANDERS, *a German woman*
HORST ANDERS, *her husband*
STEPAN IVANOV, *a Russian colonel*
JEHUDA KARP, *a Warsaw Jew*
GITTA, *a Berliner*
HALSKE, *a pianist*
OSSIP, MIHAIL, *and* PIOTR, *three Russian officers*
MARTIN, *a child*

PLACE: Berlin
TIME: Spring, 1945

WHEN THE WAR WAS OVER

ACT ONE

SCENE I

A washhouse in a cellar.

The sounds of martial music. AGNES *sits with some sewing, which she has let fall in her lap. Everyone is listening.* GITTA *stands at the cellar window, peeking out into the street.* HORST *stands to one side with an axe in his left hand; his right arm ends at the elbow; he is wearing a uniform, but without insignia and without a belt. The sound of the endless shuffling of marching feet can be heard in the street outside.*

Only the little boy, MARTIN, *goes on sleeping.*

GITTA. Here come some more. [*Pause. Band music.*] Tanks and flame-throwers, too. [*Pause. Band music.*] Mongolians! [*Pause. Band music.*]

AGNES [*face front, as if to herself*]. "That was a bitter time. From morning till night we heard nothing but the sounds of marching feet—the troops of the victor. The city had fallen. The enemy was here. His pennants fluttered against the dark sky like streamers of blood. It was noon on a day in spring; it was May, but the sky was dark with ashes and smoke, and the pale rays of the sun couldn't reach the earth. The streets were full of the bodies of dead soldiers, the enemy's and our own—and suddenly there was no difference between them. Others hung from the trees— because they had chosen not to go on fighting. There was still some scattered blind sniping from rooftops, but in a few hours the war—the damned war—would have come to an end." [*Pause. Sound of marching feet.*] "But the fear was not at an end." [*Pause. Sound of marching*

107

feet.] "One morning—a Wednesday—Agnes had to leave
the cellar; there was no more water—and the child was
weak from thirst. Agnes wrapped an ugly old kerchief
around her head—so that she would not look attractive
to the Russians—picked up a bucket, and went out. But
the filled bucket was so heavy she could scarcely carry it
back; she took the kerchief off her head and wrapped it
around her hand to keep the wire handle from cutting her
fingers. So she returned, careful not to spill the precious
water, scarcely seeing what went on around her. In the
garden she set the bucket down again, suddenly startled
as she saw the man standing in hiding in the deep shade
of the fir trees—her husband. Agnes could not believe her
eyes. He was alive. He took up the bucket, and together
they went into the house, down into this very cellar."
[*Pause. The music grows fainter.*]

GITTA. They're going on toward the Brandenburg Gate.

GITTA *comes back from the window.* AGNES *takes up her
sewing again.* HORST *taps the wall in his far corner.*

HORST. If it keeps on raining a couple more days, we can
row out of here. . . . It's starting to seep in back there.

AGNES. Water?

HORST. If it were only the water . . .

GITTA [*sits beside* AGNES]. What are you making?

HORST. A fine mess! And everything stinks of decay. . . .

GITTA. You're going to embroider the name here?

AGNES. It's best to be on the safe side.

GITTA. "Martin Anders, Berlin Zehlendorf, born: 1941." Ah
. . . that's sweet. Is that all?

AGNES. I've got time.

GITTA. What for?

*Sounds of a balalaika are heard, but the people on stage
seem accustomed to it.*

HORST. The hell of it is that I haven't got a business suit!
If I could only have thought of that! Not a single pair of
pants or a coat that isn't scorched . . . [*Pause. Balalaika.*]
I'll die down here in this miserable hole. Like a rat.

GITTA. Did you hear the story about my brother Günther?
It was a case something like this. Hidden for three years,

and all of us who knew about it putting our lives in danger
every minute. For what? Twice they searched our house.
And then all the shifting about with the food—because
Günther didn't have a ration card. It was hardest, of
course, for the child. Not a word! That was our one order.
Not even to our closest friends. "I'll hold out," Günther
kept saying. But what about the child? He went swimming
at the lake, went to the concert—knowing every moment
that his father was hiding in the cellar, crouching behind
the coalbin—knowing he must never show a sign. And
then! At last the liberation! And Günther, he couldn't
wait, of course—you remember what he was like—he ran
right out in the street, the first time in three years. He
wanted to embrace the whole army—after all, he saw the
soldiers embracing his own child—he got all mixed up
with them all; naturally, they were all drunk—they didn't
understand a word he said: a rifle-butt on top of the head,
and there he lay. [*Pause. Balalaika.*] Just you be satisfied,
Horst, that at least you're alive.

HORST. Like a rat in a trap.

GITTA. You two have found each other. Imagine! It's just
like a miracle.

AGNES. That's what I say, too.

GITTA. If only I knew where Otto was . . . [*Noise. Laughter. They look up at the ceiling.*] How many are there up
there? [AGNES *shrugs.*] Since last night?

HORST *listens at the wall.*

AGNES. You can't hear their footsteps, Horst if they go into
the living room. [*To* GITTA.] In the hall, you can hear
every boot. It's enough to drive you insane. Same thing
in the kitchen. But in the living room, where the thick
carpet is—I hadn't thought about that. All night long,
we couldn't tell if they were still there or not. We didn't
close our eyes.

Laughter and singing.

GITTA. And you think they don't suspect that anyone's in
the house?

HORST *strikes the wall with his axe.*

AGNES. Stop that.

HORST. Don't you hear?

AGNES. There's no sense in that, Horst. That won't change anything.

HORST. Filth!

AGNES. If they hear that, they'll be down here. For sure.

HORST. All night last night.

AGNES. As long as they're dancing, they're not doing something else.

HORST. There! There!

AGNES. Horst . . . ?

HORST. There! Everywhere!

AGNES. Please!

HORST. Rats—the rats——

AGNES [*turns pale*]. Rats?

Horst listens at the wall.

GITTA. If Otto is set free—I am convinced he's still alive—and if he doesn't find me at home, then he'll go to my parents. I'm sure of that. If he gets through. And if we get through. But it's nonsense just to go on waiting and waiting—day after day.

HORST. They come down from up there. Where we used to keep the supplies. It's swarming with them.

AGNES. Rats . . . ?

HORST. What's the matter? You're white as a sheet——

AGNES. Nothing.

HORST. Just over a couple of rats?

AGNES. Please—be quiet.

HORST. You know what they're like. They're always around supplies—and corpses.

AGNES. Stop it!

HORST. What's the matter?

Renewed, louder noise; they look up, waiting, until it's quiet again.

AGNES. I'm so glad that the child at least can sleep through it all.

Renewed noise. Balalaika.

GITTA. And you're sure, Horst, that your sister still has a man's suit of clothes?

HORST. Who can be sure of anything?

GITTA. Well, I mean—*fairly* sure. If I get through to Potsdam, I'll get it for you—you wait. Without you two, I'd be as good as dead.

HORST. I haven't asked you to do it.

GITTA. Why do you keep saying that?

HORST. It's not my way, to send other people on my errands. Personal errands. You can believe that, Gitta. I've never asked anybody to stick out his neck for me—never before.

GITTA. I'm not thinking of it that way.

HORST. If it weren't for this damned arm . . .

GITTA. Horst, you've got to forget about that!

A shot is heard—then another and another.

HORST. They're firing at bottles again. Or at something. God knows what.

GITTA. After all, I was only asking. If I get to Potsdam and your sister doesn't have a suit—well, I'll steal one, on my own account. But I don't have to go all the way to Potsdam for that. It's all luck, anyway. I'll try anything, if there's some point to it. The main thing is to get out of here!

HORST. I agree with that.

GITTA. As soon as possible!

HORST. As soon as I can get my hands on a suit! That's what I've been saying all along—away from here, away from these Russian swine!

AGNES [*looks at him in surprise*]. You say that too?

HORST. I really don't understand what you see in those people!

AGNES. Me?

HORST. Yes.

AGNES. I don't even know them. All I know is your stories about them. About your furlough—in your letters. Your Christmas Eve with those Russian peasants on their farm. It sounded so lovely!——

HORST. That was then.

AGNES. Wonderful people! That's what you said.

HORST. In the first year, maybe.

AGNES. As long as the war lasted.

HORST. What do you mean by that?

AGNES *turns back to her work.*

GITTA. Maybe I can find a bike, too.

AGNES. "Russian swine"—that reminds me of "Jew swine" and all the other things our own swine have said—and done.

HORST. What are you trying to say?

AGNES. It's been a long time since we've seen each other, Horst—over two years. [*She moves toward him.*] Horst . . . ? [*He doesn't move.*] Two years is a long time. . . . But we haven't changed, Horst, we'll come to understand each other again. You hear?

A sudden sharp knock at the door. They freeze, staring at each other.

GITTA. My God!

Sounds of another, adjoining cellar door being rattled, then kicked open violently. Curses in Russian. MARTIN wakes up; AGNES picks him up. Renewed knocking on their door.

AGNES. Who's there?

AGNES *signals to the others to hide themselves. She gives them the child, and they disappear into the shadows.*

AGNES. What do you want? [*She opens the door.*]

JEHUDA, *a young man in Russian uniform stumbles in. He is rather drunk and is now confused and almost speechless at the sight of* AGNES.

AGNES. What are you looking for?

JEHUDA. Madam . . .

AGNES. Do you speak German?

JEHUDA. Madam—I have not wished—I have thought there was nobodys in the house. . . .

AGNES. What?

JEHUDA. Nobodys in the house—this was what I have thinking.

AGNES. You're looking for wine?

JEHUDA. Shalom . . .

AGNES. What's that?

JEHUDA. Shalom . . . I am wishing for shalom, which is to say, "peace." Twenty weeks without house, carrying of the rifles—madam can not imagine. It is all to me so happy—this house of yours, madam, it is a palace. And

the madam must have no fear. No fear. I will make nothing "kaput" in the house. Understand? The war is dead!
The war is forgotten! No man must die——

AGNES. Take these bottles.

JEHUDA. Madam?

AGNES. Our last ones.

JEHUDA. Madam, you are a good person! I am a good person,
too! We are all good persons, eh?

AGNES. You can carry them better in your arms.

JEHUDA. Comrade Commander will laugh! He will say:
"Tovarich, this is great day!"

AGNES [continuing to hand him bottles]. Yes—and then the
others like this.

JEHUDA. I have honor, madam. I have no wine—I have great
thirst—but I am a man of honor.

AGNES. I understand.

JEHUDA. Where there is man, there is thirst. [AGNES holds
the door open for him.] My name is Jehuda Karp. I am
a Jew, but I am also a patriot——

AGNES. Yes, I understand.

JEHUDA. You, madam, understand all. Alles! [She starts to
close the door behind him, but he stumbles back in, almost
dropping the bottles.] Madam . . . ?

AGNES. Yes?

JEHUDA. Will madam desire to come upstairs to us? We are
all officers. Except me. I am only orderly. But the officers
are all fine men—all gentlemen. They all enjoy to dance.
. . . Madam does not believe me? Madam believes me to
be an animal . . . ? Madam will not come up?

AGNES. No.

JEHUDA. Comrade Commander will be very sad.

AGNES. Don't say anything to him about me. Here—take
the wine; the gentlemen are waiting for it. And don't
stumble on the stairway!

JEHUDA. Comrade Commander will be so very, very unhappy.

He goes on out. AGNES *locks the door behind him. The others
come out of hiding.*

AGNES. Well, now they all know that I'm here.

GITTA. Why did you let him in?

AGNES. Did you want him to break down the door?

HORST. I should have killed the bastard.

AGNES. Don't talk nonsense.

GITTA. If they come down here, I'll bite a vein in two—I swear it! I won't go through that a second time. Not for anything in the world! Let them shoot me, if they want to—but not that! [*Loud noise from above.*] Listen!

HORST. Now they've got the wine.

GITTA. And the information.

Loud burst of noise. Balalaika.

AGNES. All right—go. Quickly.

GITTA. What do you mean?

AGNES. And quietly! Here is some bread, Martin, but only eat it when you're hungry. Right? And stay with Gitta, you hear? No one will see you. Hide behind the cellar stairs, and when he comes back down, I'll let him in—and then, as soon as I've closed the door behind him, out!

GITTA. What if they all come down?

AGNES. So much the better. I'll keep them all in here until you get away.

GITTA. And you?

AGNES [*kneels before* MARTIN]. Martin, we'll see each other again——

MARTIN. I know, Mama.

AGNES [*crying, kisses him and then stands up*]. All right—go!

GITTA. And you?

AGNES. We'll come as soon as we can. As soon as Horst can find a suit.

GITTA. I'll try my best. . . .

AGNES [*opens the door*]. Sssh!

GITTA *slips out with* MARTIN. AGNES *locks the door, then stands with the key in her hand.*

AGNES. I hope I'm right. . . .

HORST. What do you mean?

AGNES [*face front, as if to herself*]. "Martin Anders, born 1941, Berlin Zehlendorf, seen for the last time alive on this Friday; lost in the twilight; wandering in the ruins of the night; fallen into a bomb crater where no one heard his cries; lost for six weeks; his body found by a dog; four years of age." [*She covers her face with her hands.*]

HORST. What is it? Agnes?

AGNES [*she controls herself*]. Where's the gray chest?

HORST. Why?

AGNES. Oh, here it is—never mind——

HORST. It's shameful that this woman has to go to Potsdam for my sake. For a suit. Everyone has to do everything for me now.

AGNES. Here's your bathrobe.

HORST. What about it?

AGNES. Put it on.

HORST. Now?

AGNES. So they can't see your uniform. And put the axe away. Horst—please. It's nonsense, believe me. They'll simply shoot you down.

HORST. I can't get used to it. . . .

AGNES. What?

HORST. Everybody else doing things for me. In combat, I was never helpless, I'll tell you that. Even in the tightest spots. A man can always defend himself somehow—in some way—but now that I don't have an arm any more . . . [*He has slipped on the bathrobe.*] Can you tie this for me? [AGNES *ties the sash.*] Thanks. What do you have in mind here? [*She listens.*] They're quiet now.

AGNES. Did I lock the door?

HORST. Just now.

AGNES. When they come back, you hide yourself——

HORST. And you?

AGNES. No matter what happens, they mustn't see you! [*She listens at the wall.*]

HORST. We're both going to croak down here anyway!

Balalaika. Singing.

AGNES. Have you got a cigarette? [HORST *gives her one.*] Maybe we'll get through this yet. When I think of all I've lived through here in this cellar! You know, we're still lucky, compared to other people.

HORST. Perhaps.

AGNES. That time at Sylt—remember? You always told me I was lucky—a Sunday child. Particularly during those four weeks. The way you had come back from France, and the war seemed as though it were over. I got to know you in that robe. You know what? When I think about that, today . . . [HORST *brings the cinder-box to her.*] What's this for?

HORST. Ashes.

AGNES. What for?

HORST. To smear your face with. What else?

AGNES. I don't intend to.

HORST. Agnes——

AGNES. I'm not a pig. Why should I make myself filthy and try to look like one? [HORST *looks at her, motionless.*] Ask Gitta how much the ashes helped her! Five of them came down in the cellar—she tried to defend herself, but they had a knife. To cut open her slacks, you see—they didn't understand about zippers. What could she do? Against five of them who were drunk. At least she saved her slacks —the last pair she had. [AGNES *crushes out her cigarette.*] Then an officer came—or, at any rate, a soldier who was not as drunk as the others. And then when Gitta showed him what had happened—right under his nose, so to speak—well, naturally, he ordered the rest of them out. And then he became Number Six. Despite the ashes on her face. [AGNES *rises and stands by the window.*] What do you expect? [*She comes back, sees the cigarette half, picks it up, blows it clean.*] Why are you looking at me like that? [HORST *lights her cigarette for her.*] Our last cigarettes! No sense throwing them on the floor. . . .

HORST. I wasn't thinking of that.

AGNES. What then?

HORST [*sits beside her*]. Agnes, I have a right to ask you this. Believe me. Without your becoming upset.

AGNES. What?

HORST. We're all only human. I mean—what I started to ask you yesterday . . . if you still loved me, the same as before. I don't want you to talk about what has happened. Just "yes" or "no."

AGNES. Nothing has happened, Horst.

HORST. Nothing . . . ?

AGNES. I know you don't believe that.

HORST. Two years is a long time.

AGNES. Oh, yes, indeed! When you never know who's going to live to see tomorrow. . . . Why don't you believe me? A lot has happened here, that's very true, and I would never condemn any woman for what she did then. I never knew whether you were alive or dead. There's no point in

talking about truth or virtue—it was horrible, that's all—
everything was different—I can't explain. I just wanted to
live. I didn't want to go to the dogs. . . .

HORST. Agnes!

AGNES. Do you understand what I'm saying? Without the
hope that you would return someday . . . [*A knock.
They listen—silent. Louder banging on the door.*] One
moment!

> HORST *hides.* AGNES *opens the door.* JEHUDA *enters.*

JEHUDA. Madam——

AGNES. What is it?

JEHUDA. Comrade Commander——

AGNES. You want some more wine?

JEHUDA. Not wine. We want madam.

AGNES. Stop that!

JEHUDA. Oh, not me. Comrade Commander.

AGNES. I don't need your arm.

JEHUDA. Yes—*ja*—a need!

> AGNES *moves aside.*

AGNES. What are the orders?

JEHUDA. Orders? What is orders? No one says orders. The
war is forgotten. Orders? Comrade Commander wants to
seeing the madam. . . .

AGNES. Why? [JEHUDA *smiles.*] What if I don't come?

JEHUDA. Comrade Commander will be so sad. So very sad.
Comrade Commander will have to come down here in
personal.

AGNES. Here?

JEHUDA. Why waiting, madam? Upstairs is it prettier. Eh?
Carpets on the floor, madam. In the cellar is it hard; in
the cellar is it bad. I know the cellars, madam. I have been
in the cellars. [*He puts his hand on her shoulder.*] Why
waiting, madam?

AGNES. Don't touch me!

JEHUDA. Chòrt tyebyà vazmì! [The hell with you!]

> AGNES *moves away a few steps.*

AGNES. Does he speak German?

JEHUDA. Who?

AGNES. The Commandant.

JEHUDA. But naturally! Like a book. He has great love for

the books. He has such a respect for the mind. The Ninth
Symphonic of Beethoven! He has told us: no books will be
destroyed! And a German book is a lovely book. . . . He
wants to talk with you, madam.

AGNES. Is that true?

JEHUDA. Goethe, Johann Wolfgang Goethe! Marx, Karl
Marx—Hegel—Gerhart Hoiptmann—*The Weavers!* Ein-
stein—Nobel Prize! All German—all spoke German! Will
the madam come?

AGNES. But not right away. Not like this.

JEHUDA. Why not?

AGNES. In a half-hour. I must dress.

JEHUDA. Madam is young and pretty!

AGNES. Tell the gentlemen what I say: in a half-hour.

JEHUDA. Comrade Commander will be happy.

AGNES. Please. [*She opens the door.*]

JEHUDA. In a half-hour? Comrade Commander will come
down here alone if the time is past. Comrade Commander
does not wait.

JEHUDA *goes out.*

HORST. You're not going.

AGNES. What time is it now?

HORST. Agnes, this is insane——

AGNES. And if he comes down here? [*She goes to the door,
opens it, looks out.*] Martin and Gitta are gone. [*She
comes back, opens a trunk.*] If it's true that he understands German—that's the only hope now. I'm going to
talk to him.

HORST. What will you say?

AGNES. How do I know?

HORST. Don't you hear how drunk they are? Don't you hear?
[AGNES *takes out an evening gown.*] What's that for?

AGNES. I've got to make myself as attractive as possible. [*She
slips off her shoes.*] Give me the other shoes, will you?—
the black ones, with the silver clasps. They ought to be in
the trunk, too. [*She takes off her dress.*]

HORST. And if he won't listen, what then? If he simply at-
tacks you? [AGNES *stands in her white slip.*] Agnes! I
won't survive it! You understand? I won't!

AGNES. Neither one of us will.

HORST. I'll hang myself.

AGNES [*moves toward him*]. Horst? Neither one of us will. That's definite.

She takes him by the shoulders. Loud noise from above— laughter, singing. HORST stares at her. The noise grows weaker; only the balalaika continues.

AGNES. Now, let's be sensible.

HORST. Agnes—please!

AGNES. Shall we hang ourselves? Here—in this washroom? And everything up till now . . . When I think of Erika —why haven't we both ended it all long ago?

HORST. What about Erika?

AGNES. She's not at her grandparents.

HORST. But . . . ?

AGNES. I lied.

HORST. Where is she?

AGNES. Where the rats are.

HORST. Erika . . .

AGNES. A land mine. On the eleventh of February. I wanted to tell you later.

HORST. That, too.

AGNES. I'll talk with him. I'll try it. And if I can't do it, if my good luck has run out—we won't desert one another, Horst. . . . Right? We want to live as long as we can, and if we can't, if we have to go on all fours like beasts— then, no more! [*She gazes into his eyes.*] No more.

HORST. No more.

AGNES *kisses him on the forehead—a kiss like the taking of a vow, or a farewell. Loud noise from above. AGNES takes the evening dress and starts to put it on.*

AGNES. How much time do I have now?

Curtain.

SCENE II

The living room.

Four more or less drunken RUSSIAN SOLDIERS *who are entertaining themselves in the following manner:* PIOTR, *a blond*

*youngster, who is evidently the comedian of the group, sits
atop the black grand piano and strums on a balalaika, con-
tinuing to the end of the song. A brief silence ensues. Another,* Ossip, *sits on the divan gazing at his watch.*

Ossip. Polchasà? Yèsli anà nye pridyòt, tavàrishch Kamandìr,
tak ya yiyò za vòlasi privalakù. [Half an hour? If she
doesn't come, Comrade Commander, I'll drag her up here
by the hair.]

The Commandant, Stepan Ivanov, *seated in an easy chair,
does not answer; he fills his glass and drinks silently. All of
them have taken off their tunics. Another,* Mihail, *is operat-
ing the record player; he reads the label of the record he is
about to play.*

Mihail. "Drei Grossen Opper."

*He puts the record on the turntable, flips the switch. Mean-
while, he goes through the record collection, takes one out,
holds it up, and* Ossip, *lying on the divan, fires at it with his
revolver, shattering it. This is repeated several times.*

Record Player.
>   Und der Haifisch, der hat Zähne
>   Un die trägt er im Gesicht
>   Und Macheath, der hat ein Messer
>   Doch das Messer sieht man nicht.

Shot.

>   Ach es sind des Haifischs Flossen
>   Rot, wenn dieser Blut vergiesst
>   Mackie Messer trägt 'nen Handschuh
>   Drauf man keine Untat liest.

Shot.

>   An der Themse grünem Wasser
>   Fallen plötzlich Leute um
>   Es ist weder Pest noch Cholera
>   Doch es heisst: Macheath geht um.

Shot.

>   Und das grosse Feuer in Soho
>   Sieben Kinder und ein Greis
>   In der Menge Mackie Messer, den
>   Man fragt und der nichts weiss.

Shot. But this one misses; the record is untouched. Laughter.

*They look to see where it has struck and find the bullet hole
in the door, right. PIOTR points with his finger; OSSIP gets
up, swaying unsteadily, and they open the door—which
opens directly into midair. They draw back involuntarily from
the gaping ruins, while the record plays itself out.*

> Und die minderjährge Witwe
> Deren Namen jeder weiss,
> Wachte auf und war geschändet—
> Mackie, welches war dein Preis?

Silence.

STEPAN. Berlin—— [*He remains seated.*] Nazàd, nazàd!
Dver astànyetsa zapertòy. [Back, back! That door will be
kept locked.]

*During this, AGNES has entered. She is wearing a long even-
ing dress and a wrap of white fur. At first, they don't see her.
PIOTR, turning back from having closed the door, is the first
to notice her.*

PIOTR. Ah . . . lady! Beautiful lady!

AGNES. Good evening, gentlemen. I hope I'm not intruding.

STEPAN *rises.* PIOTR *seats himself quickly at the piano and
begins to play the "Horst Wessel Song." OSSIP draws his
knife and, creeping around behind the piano, cuts the wires
one by one. The song stops.*

AGNES. I was invited here. My name is Anders, Agnes Anders. I was told the Commandant would like to speak with
me.

PIOTR. Gracious lady!

AGNES. Please—don't.

PIOTR. Oho!

AGNES. Don't touch me—please!

> PIOTR *grabs hold of her dress.*

PIOTR. Zakhadìtye, tavàrischchi, zakhadìtye! [Come on in,
comrades, come on in!]

> *He lifts up her dress. She slaps his face.*

AGNES. I told you not to do that.

*Meanwhile, OSSIP, who has been firing at the records and
cutting the piano strings, moves closer; his face is red with
sudden anger; he intends to show her what she can and cannot do. He seizes her by her fur wrap.*

Ossip. Ti shto dùmayesh? Ti dùmayesh nàs mòzhna bits pa mòrdam? Ti svinyà nyemyètskaya, ti svòloch girmànskaya! [What do you think? You think you can hit us in the face, you German pig, you German bitch!]

Ossip *lifts up her skirt again. She slaps him in the face also. He presses his revolver against her breast. She closes her eyes.* Stepan *strikes the revolver from his hand, while the other two pull* Ossip *back. During the confusion,* Jehuda *enters the room.*

Stepan. Proch revòlver! [Put the revolver away!]

Ossip [*talking to* Agnes]. Kto pabyedìtyel, ti ìli ya? [Who won the war, you or me?]

Stepan. Vìkintye yevo. [Throw him out.]

Ossip. Nyemyètskaya svinyà, svòloch girmànskaya! [German pig, German bitch!]

Stepan. Malchàts! [Silence!]

Agnes *looks at* Jehuda.

Agnes. Tell the gentlemen I'd like to speak to the Commandant—alone.

Stepan. Malchàts! Moy prikàz: nyemyèdlina razaidìtyes. Kto ètu zhènshchinu pasmyèyet trònuts bùdyet rastrèlyen na myèstye. [Silence! I order you to get out of here at once. Whoever dares touch this woman will be shot on the spot.]

They obey sullenly and go out of the room, one by one. Jehuda, *as the last to leave, closes the sliding doors behind him.* Agnes *and* Stepan *are left alone.*

Agnes. Thank you. [Stepan *gestures toward a chair.*] I'd rather stand. [Stepan *puts on his tunic.*] If you are the Commandant—I assume the orderly wasn't lying . . . If it were up to me, of course, I would never have come. You have taken over our house; war is war, and I have no right to demand anything here, I understand that quite clearly—— [Stepan *offers her a cigarette.*] Thank you— no. [Stepan *takes a cigarette for himself.*] I don't know why you have invited me here. It looks like—well, I can imagine, of course. . . . You are men, and I am a woman, unable to defend myself. . . . If that is your will, I'll simply bite through one of my veins and bleed to death— that's all you'll accomplish. [Stepan *lights his cigarette.*] I'm here to listen to whatever you have to say. [Stepan, *observing her, smiles.*] I suppose I can understand your silence, your suspicion—after all that has happened in these last few years. I speak a language, I know, which must fill you with hate and disgust. I really don't know what I can say to you. As long as I speak this language, all you will hear in my words is the fact that I am German. . . . [STEPAN *smokes in silence.*] Well—I am a German. Yes. [STEPAN *smokes silently.*] And my husband was on the Eastern front. Your enemy. But I could show you his letters, the ones he wrote to me from the Ukraine. There in the writing desk, where you're sitting, a whole bundle of them. . . . If you read them, what he wrote then, maybe you could believe me, that we too are not just the Enemy, without distinction. There are no races. I have never believed in that. If I did, I wouldn't be standing here now, before a Russian officer—knowing, as I do, what happened to my friend Gitta. And all the other things that have happened, too—all this beastliness—a person like Günther, a man who had longed for your arrival, who—coming out of the cellar—is struck down by a rifle-butt, and nobody thinks a thing about it! Really—— [STEPAN *smokes.*] Why is that? Why should it be? [STEPAN *smokes in silence.*] I know, you must be thinking of many others, too. Maybe even you feel very differently about all this—and you are smiling at me in secret. I am not a very deep thinker, I know! But yet I feel that things must not go on this way . . . my God! with all these stupid speeches and slogans, all this insanity about races and peoples—as though we all weren't flesh and blood, just human beings of flesh and blood, you and I. . . . [STEPAN *rises, goes to the window, and throws his cigarette butt out.*] Why don't you say something to me? [*She sits.* STEPAN *remains at the window, sitting on the ledge, watching her.*] As a child I lived for a long time in China. My father worked for North German Lloyd Lines. Once when I was eleven—I got lost and found myself standing all alone in a rice field, nothing but the tall grass all around. I have never felt greater terror—the sudden feeling that I was all alone on this planet—me—two days and two nights I spent like this, cloudless, sun and moon, nothing but grass and water. . . . Finally a Chinese found me, by chance, a tramp, to whom I could not speak a word, not a name, not a syllable he could understand. But at that moment he didn't strike me as strange, as foreign, this man who came toward me through the high grass. . . . Up until then I had only noticed that their eyes were different from ours, different skin, a shaved skull, but now— and this fellow was nothing exceptional; he got a sizable ransom from my father for rescuing me!—still, he was a man, a being like myself. . . . I don't know if you understand what I'm saying. I can still see that fellow as he came through the tall grass—first his bald head, then his arms, and his whole thin body. . . . If a man cries out, if he bleeds—suddenly I am no longer interested in the shape of his nose, his language, his face, the place of his birth. [STEPAN *turns and goes to the piano.*] I'm not sure what you think of this question. [STEPAN *brings a bottle and two glasses.*] If you would just read the letters—there in the writing desk—maybe you could believe that here, too, in Germany there are human beings, and you wouldn't just treat me with silence—the way one treats an animal with silence. What am I saying: an animal? A thing! [STEPAN *offers her a full glass.*] No—thank you very much.

STEPAN. Varry goot!

AGNES. No, thanks. I know that brand. [STEPAN *touches her glass with his and waits.*] Really—no. You must excuse me. [*He drinks.* AGNES *holds the full glass.*] Why are you silent? Why don't you say what you are thinking? You wanted me to come . . . ! I know. You thought: A woman—an adventure! That's always the way we treat the enemy! And then I come here and ask you to treat me as a human being—and you smile! . . . Why not? After all you must have experienced at the hands of people who speak my language! Or have you sworn never to exchange a word with us? Well, perhaps you want a proof of the person who stands before you—— [*She sets her glass aside.*] What if I give you some proof? [STEPAN *refills his glass.*] Suppose I give you all my trust, suppose I show you that I place our fate entirely in your hands— without deception, without reserve—will you believe then that the rest I have told you is also true? Yes? Suppose I

say—it is up to me to take the first step toward confidence
and trust, I know—suppose I say to you very frankly, my
husband is . . . [*She hesitates.* STEPAN *drinks.*] My husband is hiding in the cellar beneath us. [STEPAN *wipes his
mouth with his hand.*] My husband is a captain. That is
to say, he was. Two years ago, at Stalingrad, he was taken
prisoner—I don't know where the camp was. He never
talks about it. I never even knew, then, that he was alive.
. . . The day before yesterday, when I was fetching water,
suddenly there he was in the garden. He said he'd been
hiding under the fir trees for the whole night because he
didn't know who might be in the house—or whether I was
still alive. You can imagine how I felt! He had lost his
right arm, but otherwise . . . He had escaped from the
prison a month ago, he said, during a transfer. [STEPAN
watches her in silence.] I can say no more. [STEPAN *fills
his glass for the third time.*] If there were no Horst, I don't
know how I could have borne these last years—without
the knowledge that there were other men out there like
Horst—no angels, mind you, but men, men who didn't go
to the dogs, men like Horst, who finally simply had to
defend themselves—and without this knowledge—and
knowing such a person oneself . . . Oh, he's not the only
one, God knows, but one that I know of for sure—and
without that knowledge, I don't see how a person could
bear to live in such a world as this! And that's why I have
the courage to stand here and ask that you treat us as
human beings—— [STEPAN *drinks.*] Would you like us
to leave the house? Does our presence disturb you? Or
could we at least remain in the cellar? Just tell me what's
going to happen. [STEPAN *empties his glass.*] Yes or no?
[*He is silent. She breaks down crying.*] My God in Heaven!
What do you want from me? Must I throw myself on my
knees to make you answer? What have I done to you?
[STEPAN *arises uneasily and with an expression of surprise
and pity.*] Don't pretend! I know you understand German!
STEPAN. Jehuda?
AGNES. Or else your orderly lied to me!
STEPAN. Jehuda? Jehuda!
STEPAN *goes to the door and opens it. We hear the balalaika
again. Singing.*

AGNES. Dogs! Common curs! [*She runs to the other door, from which she had entered, finds it locked, runs to the third door, which opens in midair, rattles it in vain.*] Not even this one!

STEPAN *comes back with* JEHUDA, *who is wearing an apron and carrying a frying pan and a dish towel. Meanwhile,* AGNES *has seen the revolver, which is lying on the floor. She picks it up quickly and hides it under her fur wrap.*

AGNES. You've lured me into a trap! He doesn't understand one word! Not one word! It was all a lie!

JEHUDA. Madam——

AGNES. You miserable dog, you!

JEHUDA. Madam does not understand a little joke?

AGNES. To hell with your jokes!

JEHUDA. Comrade Commander says he has had great joy of madam.

AGNES. Thank you.

JEHUDA. Great, great joy, says Comrade Commander. Madam shall speech again, and I shall translate.

AGNES. What?

JEHUDA. All.

STEPAN *gestures toward a chair.* AGNES *remains standing.*

AGNES. Ask him how long the gentlemen are going to stay in our house.

JEHUDA. Anà khòchit znats skòlka mi yishchò zdyès astànyemsa. [*She wants to know how much longer we'll be staying here.*]

STEPAN. Nyeznàyu. [*I don't know.*]

JEHUDA. Anà nas bayìtsa. [*She's afraid of us.*]

STEPAN. Nyedyèli trì, chetìri . . . [*About three or four weeks . . .*]

JEHUDA [*turns back to* AGNES]. Comrade Commander knows not. Comrade Commander says three weeks, four—he knows not.

AGNES. Tell the Colonel that I will make him the following offer——

She stops as the other SOLDIERS *appear in the door. She waits till* STEPAN *notices them, too.*

STEPAN. Zakròy dvèr! [*Shut the door.*]

The door is slammed shut.

AGNES. I make the following offer: I will do whatever he asks of me, I will be his mistress—no, don't say that!

JEHUDA. What does madam wish?

AGNES. Say—I will drink with him—every evening, if he wishes it. Under two conditions. First: all the others must leave our house. The Colonel must guarantee it. And second: the Colonel can choose the hour, but he must pledge not to try to find out what I do during the rest of my time. . . . Please—translate that.

JEHUDA. With great pleasure, madam.

AGNES. If I am not on the spot at the hour agreed upon, of course, then he can come and get me. But if I keep my word, then I will expect him to keep his. As an officer.

JEHUDA. Anà dyèlayit predlazhèniye: vopyèrvikh . . . [She's making an offer: first . . .] [The rest is unintelligible; we can see him ticking off the conditions on his fingers. A lengthy whispered conversation ensues.]

STEPAN. Kharashò. [Good.] [JEHUDA turns back to AGNES. STEPAN. adds.] Ya devòlyen. [I'm satisfied.]

JEHUDA. Comrade Commander wishes to say that he is in complete agreeable with madam. [He bows and exits.]

STEPAN and AGNES are alone. STEPAN takes the filled glass that AGNES has set aside and hands it to her. He wishes to touch glasses. First he introduces himself.

STEPAN. Ivanov. Stepan Ivanov.

AGNES. Agnes . . . [She faints.]

STEPAN. Jehuda! Jehuda! [JEHUDA hurries back in.] Anà vòbmarok upàla! [She's fainted!]

JEHUDA. Èta gòled. [It's from hunger.]

STEPAN and JEHUDA pick her up and put her in a half-sitting, half-recumbent position on the divan. Again the balalaika is heard through the open sliding doors. They cover AGNES with an officer's overcoat. STEPAN observes her for a while, then gives JEHUDA a sign to straighten the room and pick up the pieces of broken records. STEPAN helps too; they kneel on the carpet together—one of them bumps the table and a bottle falls and breaks. AGNES opens her eyes without moving; the kneeling men, working quietly, do not see her eyes open. We see the gun in her hand. STEPAN rises. AGNES closes her eyes. JEHUDA tiptoes out, carrying a pan full of

broken fragments. STEPAN, *alone with the sleeping woman,
watches her in silence. Then he decides to continue clean-
ing up. He kneels directly in front of the sofa. Suddenly he
straightens up with an exclamation of pain.* AGNES *starts up
involuntarily to a sitting position; they look at one another.*
STEPAN *smiles at her slowly.*

AGNES. You're bleeding. . . . Look, where you've bled on
the rug . . . ! Don't you understand what I'm saying?
Your hand, Ivanov, look at your left hand!

STEPAN. Ivanov. Stepan Ivanov.

AGNES. Yes. Stepan Ivanov, you're bleeding. . . .

Curtain.

ACT TWO

SCENE I

The washhouse.

HORST *is standing at the window. Sunset.* AGNES *is preparing his supper. There is a long silence.*

HORST. Tomorrow it will be exactly three weeks. [*Pause.*]

AGNES. There was some white bread in the store today. . . . [*Pause.*]

HORST. If a man could only get a breath of fresh air!

AGNES *stops in her activities.*

AGNES [*face front*]. "Yesterday Agnes went out. At seven o'clock, the hour at which she always went out, he was already waiting—in his overcoat and cap. Stepan had procured a car, a Mercedes, and they drove off together in it. Grünewald, Schlachtersee, the last sun on the pine trees. On the shores of the Wannsee, they got out; she walked through the deep sand in her black pumps; she wore an evening dress; together they took a small boat. The sun was down, but the evening was warm, and they spent two hours out there on the water. He put his coat around Agnes's shoulders, and it smelled of gasoline, of tobacco, of sweat and oil. It was lovely."

HORST *leaves the window.*

HORST. If a man could only get a breath of fresh air!

AGNES *passes him a plate.*

AGNES. People are swimming in the Wannsee already. And everywhere the grass is growing over the ruins. As though nothing had happened. In Kladow, where we used to play golf—a couple of guns and some rusty antiaircraft searchlights—otherwise nothing. The clubhouse has been blown up—that's all.

HORST. How do you know all this?

AGNES. What?

HORST. How it looks now in Kladow.

AGNES. Gitta and I were there in February, looking for wood.

HORST. And that people are already swimming in the Wannsee?

AGNES. I imagine they are. Why not? I can picture it—after all, it's the end of May! [A *piano tuner can be heard at work*.] Why do you shake your head?

HORST. There he goes again!

AGNES. Don't listen.

HORST. It's driving me crazy! The whole damned day! And then Mozart!

AGNES. Your food is ready.

HORST. The Piano Concerto in D minor. [*He sits down.*]

AGNES. I don't understand Gitta. To throw this note through the window like that—and not a word about Martin— she must know how much I worry about him! Not a line——

HORST. Why don't you eat?

AGNES. I can't.

HORST. You're growing more miserable all the time, Agnes. That's not good.

AGNES. Don't worry about me—really——

HORST. Maybe you can get something better upstairs.

AGNES [*turns sharply*]. What do you take me for?

HORST. A person has got to stay alive . . .

AGNES. I asked you a question.

HORST. Good Lord!——

AGNES. Do you think that I'm some kind of a whore? [*She sobs.*]

HORST. What *is* this?

AGNES. Don't touch me!

HORST. Don't start crying again.

AGNES. To think that you can be so common!

HORST. Agnes, for Heaven's sake, what have I said? Don't take everything so personally—— [*She moves away from him.*] That's just what I'm telling you: Your nerves are all shot because you won't eat properly. You're growing thinner every day. I can see it.

AGNES [*sits down and takes off her shoes*]. What time is it now?

HORST. Twenty minutes to seven. Twenty-one minutes, to be exact.

AGNES slips on the black shoes.

AGNES. That would be foolish of me, to eat everything up when I have no need of it. You can enjoy every bite.

HORST. When my suit comes, we won't need any more supplies. Just what we can carry in our pockets. . . .

AGNES. How do you know your suit is coming?

HORST. If Gitta says a thing . . . Here: "Suit coming Thursday." . . . I ask you—— [AGNES *is silent.*] Really, you're funny, Agnes. For three weeks now we've been waiting in this lousy cellar, and now the waiting is almost over and you——

AGNES picks up her evening dress.

AGNES. Leave here now? Where's the sense in that?

HORST. I don't understand you.

AGNES. Nothing's happening to us here. Naturally, life here in this cellar, away from the sun . . . But they won't stay here forever, and when they go, we'll have our house. There's always that. It's a matter of a few days more or less. If we run off now, we have nothing. Not even a roof over our heads . . . We've got to consider all sides of the question.

HORST. Do you mean you want to stay here?

AGNES. Our food will last us at least another week.

HORST. As long as you don't eat a bite—yes.

AGNES. Well, I just don't want to run off into—nothingness. Head over heels. Maybe in another week the house will be empty!

HORST. Maybe.

AGNES. Well, then . . .

HORST. And maybe not.

AGNES goes behind a screen to change her dress.

AGNES. You're always complaining that you're bored to death, but when I bring you books, you don't want to read them.

HORST. Books . . .

AGNES. You used to read all the time.

HORST. *Bismarck, His Life and Work.*

AGNES. I couldn't pick and choose, I tell you. I just had to grab what was near the door.

HORST. *The Most Famous Quotations from Classical Antiquity.* "Odysseus returns to Ithaca. Odysseus as a beggar in the great hall. Odysseus scorned. Night and morning in the palace"——

AGNES. There are others there.

HORST. We used to crack jokes about that stuff in school. *Anna Karenina . . . People without Land . . . Riding Instructions for a Dear One . . . The Decline of the West . . . Heart in the Body . . . Observations of a Nonpolitical Man . . .* by Thomas Mann . . . hmmm . . . *Love Letters of Three Centuries . . .* you gave me this one.

AGNES. Me? [*She comes out in her evening dress, which is not yet hooked up. She is arranging her hair while holding the hair-clasp in her teeth.*]

HORST. "To my darling Horst, after our first ball at the Hermitage, your happy Agnes."

AGNES. What time is it now?

HORST. Quarter to seven. The Colonel has trained you to be punctual, I'll say that for him. [AGNES *turns so that he can hook up the back of her dress.*] Why won't you ever tell me what he looks like?

AGNES. You know what Russians look like.

HORST. Every day you tell me less and less. . . . The first time it was different, you know, when you came back down here; you were upset, but you told me all about it. Your whole conversation. And now?

AGNES [*feels the back of her dress*]. Thanks. [*She combs her hair before a mirror.*]

HORST. Your discussions of Heine, of Karl Marx, and all the others we've been forbidden to read—for instance, that business about Ossietzky, all those names we've never even heard of. . . . You know, it's really something, when you stop to think about it, that a Russian knows more about these things than we do. . . . And we, always thinking about wolves on the steppes whenever anybody mentions Russia—I've done it myself! And God knows I spent my

share of time on the Eastern front, too! I met a lot of
men there, different from us, different people, but damned
fine people, too. Only we couldn't talk to them. They
would put milk on the table for us, and then, when they
left the room, we'd put our heads together and wonder,
"What are they thinking?" We were always suspicious—
just like today. All because of the damned language! And
now there's a Russian here in our own house, one who
speaks perfect German, and suddenly, when you tell me
about your conversations with him . . . suddenly everything seems completely different—certain things that I
always hated, certain names that I couldn't stand . . . all
at once it appears in a different light when I listen to you
talk about it—almost a kind of glory. Seriously. [AGNES
combs her hair in silence.] Do you understand that?

AGNES. And that's why you want to leave?

HORST. But the last few times you've said less and less—
nothing at all, unless I ask.

Mozart is heard again from above.

AGNES. I find it strange, too, that you tell *me* nothing. For
two years you disappeared—and not a word about what
you did or where you were. Not since Warsaw.

HORST [*listens*]. Was that Gitta?

AGNES. What?

HORST. Didn't you hear?

AGNES. Gitta?

HORST. Someone called my name. Quite clearly.

AGNES. Gitta wouldn't come before it was dark [*She rises.*]
What time is it now? [*She starts to file her fingernails.*]
Why are you looking at me like that?

HORST. You've made yourself really very beautiful, Agnes.

AGNES. Are you blaming me for that? Once we start going
around looking like slatterns, then everything is lost. You
men can't understand that, but it's so. In Paris, in the
summer of 1940, you understood it then. [*She seats herself again at the mirror.*]

HORST. And yet you don't want to tell me what he looks
like.

AGNES. Who?

HORST. Who!

AGNES. I told you, he's a Russian. . . . And any child can

tell you what a Russian looks like. Why else do we have
pictures? Every race of people has a flag and a face. The
Jew has a hooked nose and thick lips, not to mention certain traits of character. The Englishman is thin and ath-
letic—so long as the sport suits his tastes. The Spaniard
is haughty; the Italian has an enviable singing voice, although he is lazy and superficial; the German is loyal and
profound. And the Frenchman has *esprit*, but nothing
more. . . . The Russian—just think about all the partisans you met.

HORST. I didn't meet any.

AGNES. Well, then, think about the pictures in the papers!
That's what he looks like—and on his neck he has a scar,
or maybe a birthmark, I'm not sure. [*She powders her
face.*] And now, my dear friend, are you satisfied?

*Through the cellar window there comes a hand, which
knocks on the wall, but neither of them notices it. The piano
tuner starts playing Mozart again. The hand appears again,
holding a bundle, which it lets fall. HORST sees it. He looks to
see if AGNES has noticed it, but she has not. She is still
powdering her face. After a brief hesitation, HORST makes a
quick decision, takes the bundle, and slides it under his cot.
          The piano music stops. AGNES turns to him.*

AGNES. Do you know what a kolkhoz is?

HORST. Why?

AGNES. Yesterday he talked about this kolkhoz the whole
time. [*She applies lipstick.*] You see, a kolkhoz is a group
of farmers. . . . [*She stops. Face front.*] "Three weeks
before, when Agnes had gone out for the first time, they
had sworn to one another that she would not sell her life
in shame. But what was she to do if it were love and not
shame? The fourteen steps that she went up, and the fourteen steps that she came down, night after night, and the
hours up there, where she loved, and the hours down here,
where she lied . . . what was she to do? Horst was safe
as long as he believed, and, as she always said, he believed
in order to be safe."

          They look at one another.

HORST. Why do you look at me like that?

AGNES. And you? Why are you looking at me?

HORST. You look wonderful, Agnes. Just like our first ball—at the Hermitage.

AGNES. You were going to say something else.

HORST. I don't know.

AGNES. Go on. Say it.

HORST. Do you enjoy going up there?

AGNES. Horst——

HORST. I only asked. [*She throws herself against him.*]

AGNES. Don't let me go! Never again!

HORST. Agnes?

AGNES. Hold me! Hold me!

HORST. Ssssh . . . [*He strokes her hair.*]

AGNES. Don't ever let me go again.

HORST. And what if they come down here?

AGNES. Shoot me.

HORST. Agnes . . .

AGNES. Both of us. [*She sobs against his shoulder.*]

HORST. He loves you. . . . I can understand that. Good Lord, that's no crime. If nothing has happened—I know, it was cheap of me, the first time, when you came back down. I won't make you swear an oath again.

AGNES. I've never broken my word——

HORST. Of course, you were so strange. "Don't look at me like an animal!" you shouted. So hostile. For days you didn't look me in the eye. And you must admit you didn't make it very easy for me, waiting here in this cellar three—four hours! You've got to understand how I felt, Agnes—although I promise, I'll never ask you again. I promise you. Never again. You hear? You're different now than you were that first time, believe me. You're not afraid any more—I can feel it. It hasn't been easy to believe you, but—why are you trembling . . . ? If nothing has happened up till now, then there's nothing for you to be afraid of any more; no man who loves a woman will try to force her against her will—you know that for sure.

AGNES. Shoot me! [*She takes the gun out of her fur.*] Do it! Now! Do it! [*He takes the gun out of her hand.*] Believe in me or shoot me! [*She falls to her knees.*]

HORST. What's all this . . . ? Come—stand up—come. . . . Let's try to be sensible. . . . If you don't go now—

it's obvious that I believe you—otherwise, we're lost, both of us—you hear?

AGNES [*puts her hands over her eyes*]. "If you don't go now. It's obvious that I believe you. Otherwise, we're both lost."

The Mozart is heard again from above.

HORST. Agnes, it's past seven.

Curtain.

SCENE II

The living room.

At the piano, playing Mozart, a man named HALSKE is seated. He breaks off abruptly and once more begins the piano-tuning exercises. JEHUDA, the orderly, is going to and fro preparing the evening meal.

HALSKE. Tell the Colonel I've repaired the wires that were cut. According to orders. I've replaced them with wires from my own concert grand. But that's the least of the trouble. I don't know what you gentlemen think a piano is. The whole instrument stinks of wine. [JEHUDA *goes out again.*] So these are the new conquerors of the world! Swine!——

JEHUDA returns with a bottle.

JEHUDA. I don't like to listen to the German language, but I am understanding it.

HALSKE. I say what I think—even if people understand me. [JEHUDA *looks at him.*] Piano tuning is not my profession, I assure you.

JEHUDA attaches the corkscrew to the bottle.

JEHUDA. Why is it you are not now already dead?

HALSKE. I beg your pardon?

JEHUDA. Why is it you are not now already dead?

HALSKE. Me? Dead? Why?

JEHUDA. The gentleman is used to saying as he thinks, no?

HALSKE. That's right.

JEHUDA. What then did the gentleman think as he was let to live in the long twelve years? [JEHUDA *draws the cork.*]

HALSKE. Oh, I'm not complaining. You understand me correctly. Others had to dig graves. In the pouring rain! Not me. I suppose I can't expect now that my name would mean anything to you. But there was injustice enough during those years, God knows—— [JEHUDA *sets the table*.] But what crime had I committed? I ask you. Just because my career reached its height at that time. What did Mozart have to do with the Third Reich? And what else did I do except play Mozart—in the midst of the worst bombardments, too—spring, 1943! [JEHUDA *continues his work*.] You don't believe me, eh? [JEHUDA *is silent*.] All right, then—don't.

HALSKE *tries the piano concerto again; in truth, he plays very well.* JEHUDA *polishes the glasses, testing them against the light. As the music stops once more, he continues polishing and talking.*

JEHUDA. Nineteen and forty-three . . . I was in the ghetto —in Warsaw. . . . They let the water into the canal, where I am trying to get away, and when I am coming up out of the canal to keep from drowning—there they were with the little pistols: Ta ta ta ta! One of us must get to the Russians, but how? My mother is drowned there; my father is shot before my eyes; my sister is lost— eh? So I said to the woman: "Lay me on the wagon with the corpses, I must get away!" So they laid me in the wagon among the corpses, and I am getting away. "Brothers," I said, "don't shoot, don't uncover." And then, when it is dark, I am standing up and running off. . . . [*He arranges the glasses.*]

HALSKE. I don't know why you tell me this. Me, of all people. I had nothing to do with any of that, God knows.

JEHUDA. This is happening in Warsaw.

HALSKE. Could be . . .

JEHUDA. March, nineteen and forty-three.

HALSKE. You mustn't think I condone such things just because they involved Jews. I have nothing against the Jews. In our orchestra there was a whole row of Jews—all very talented musicians—— Why are you looking at me like that . . . ? Things were different then, that's all I can say. It was Captain Anders who was in Warsaw, not me!

JEHUDA. Captain Anders?

HALSKE. Horst Anders. I am only an artist. [JEHUDA *takes out a small notebook.*] Now look—I'm no informer. I have had many dealings in this house, and these people have never done me any harm. Quite the contrary, in fact! All I mean is, our people can't move around much any more. . . .

JEHUDA makes a note.

JEHUDA. Horst Anders. Captain. Warsaw—nineteen and forty-three.

HALSKE. Look—please understand me! I didn't say the man was there then—I can't testify to it. Besides, I don't get myself involved in politics, on principle——— [STEPAN *enters.*] Colonel, the piano is tuned.

STEPAN takes off his overcoat and cap. HALSKE, after waiting in vain for an answer, bows and withdraws. STEPAN glances at the clock.

STEPAN. Gdyè nàsha slavnàya Frau? [Where is our charming Frau?]

JEHUDA shrugs and exits. STEPAN stands, studying the fully set table. Meanwhile, AGNES appears in the other door, unnoticed by him. Unable to wait, he picks up a piece of meat from the table and puts it in his mouth.

AGNES. Good appetite!

STEPAN whirls in surprise. They laugh.

STEPAN. Agnes! [*They embrace.*]

AGNES. How are you? [*She kisses him.*] Eh? [*He kisses her.*] Come—are you hungry? [*They go arm in arm toward the table.*]

STEPAN. Ya ràd shto ubezhàl. Vot tibyà, ya panimàyu. Nyèmtsyef ya nye panimàyu. Anì nyè chèstniye knàm. Da i nàshikh tavàrishchey nye panimàyu. Vaynà ikh sdyèlala zvirmì. [I'm glad I got away. Now you, I understand you. I don't understand the Germans. They're not honest with us. I don't even understand our comrades. The war has made animals out of them.]

They have seated themselves.

AGNES. Let's don't think about unpleasant things tonight, Stepan. Not while we're here together. Think about last night, on the lake———

STEPAN. The lake? Good———

AGNES. How fast can our Mercedes go?

STEPAN. Mercedes—kaput!

They laugh; AGNES *fills her plate with food.*

AGNES. I haven't been able to stop thinking about you all day long. [*She rises.*] We mustn't do that again, Stepan. To travel off into the countryside like that. You understand? While he's hiding down there in that cellar—— [*Noticing that* STEPAN *isn't eating.*] Here's the pepper. [STEPAN *takes her on his knee.*] You understand this, don't you? He's such a good man. If you could see him —down there—and here I sit on your knee! It's all so crazy! If only it weren't for the language, Stepan, you two could understand each other. I know you could. You could be friends. Often, it almost seems to me that you two are one and the same man. . . . Can you understand that? [STEPAN *takes her face in his hands.*]

STEPAN. Zachèm ti plàkala? [Why were you crying?]

AGNES. I don't know what you mean.

STEPAN. Ti zachèm plàkala? [Why were you crying?] [*He points to her eyes.*]

AGNES. Don't worry about that. Eyes sometimes look like this. But let's not talk about it any more. [*She rises and returns to her place opposite him.*]

STEPAN. Agnes?

AGNES. Stepan, how long can this go on? With us. And yet I find it so lovely, I'm so happy, somehow, that neither of us understands what the other one is saying. . . . But I do love you, Stepan, do you know that? Even when my eyes are red from weeping, I'm happy. And when you are gone, I'll never be happy again. Not like this. But don't worry about me. Even if you can't understand what I'm saying to you. Maybe it's never any different between a man and a woman, when they speak together, when words mean nothing, after all. . . . If you had not come into my life, Stepan, I would never know that life could be like this—that I could be like this, the way I am with you— so free of fear and pretense—so open and free! Do you know that? I can tell you what I could never tell any other man; you hear it, Stepan, and yet it all remains a secret— my secret. . . . You know, I don't even know who you are—only that we love each other. And you are simply

here: You are all that I can imagine. How have I deserved
this happiness? And then to think—there has never been
a lie between us. . . . [*She takes his hand.*] Stepan? [*He
is silent, gazing at her.*] Now you are here. [*They look at
one another.*] Come—you've got to eat! [*She draws away
and rises.*] If only I weren't so worried about the child!
Tomorrow it will be three weeks. Why did I just let him
leave the cellar like that? I don't understand myself any
more. And not a word from Gitta! All that fuss over that
stupid suit. . . . And suppose she does find one? What
then? [STEPAN *offers her a glass of wine.*] No. I don't want
anything to drink.

STEPAN. Agnes——

AGNES. I want to be happy without that.

STEPAN. Ti minyà nye lyùbish? [You don't love me?]

AGNES. What's the matter? Are you angry again?

STEPAN. Ti minyà nye lyùbish? [You don't love me?]

AGNES. I don't understand what you're trying to say.

STEPAN. Ìli da? [Or do you?]

AGNES. You've got to understand, Stepan, this isn't right. I
can't go back down to that cellar smelling of wine. You
can see that, can't you? Oh, God—what's right, what's
not right! I sleep with you—Stepan Ivanov, a man who
knows nothing about me except that I love him—and he
loves me—Stepan Ivanov, that's right! I long for you, each
time, I can't wait till night is here—and that makes everything right! Why hasn't Horst shot me? I love you, Stepan
—I can't change that. All these lies and tricks—I'll never
understand how I've done it. And all around us, out there
—it's all so horrible, the things that are happening. . . .
But when you hold me in your arms . . . I think of
Gitta, I think of Günther, struck down and killed. . . .
And then you kiss me, and I am silent—and happy . . .
yes, happy! And everything is right. [STEPAN *takes her by
the shoulders.*] Stepan, who am I? [*He kisses her.*] One
day you will leave me—quite suddenly. The whole night
I lay awake, thinking—it was raining in streams. Very
often I can't understand how I can sleep—and why I
don't just get up and get dressed and come to you. As
long as we are both here and alive and breathing . . .
[*She breaks away and goes to sit on the sofa.*] I know you

don't think anything bad about me. [STEPAN *stands. He offers her a cigarette.*] When Horst and I were married . . . [*He lights her cigarette.*] Really, I never wanted any other man. . . . Horst was a lieutenant then. He had just returned from France—and we really thought at that time that the war was about to end. Or maybe we just tried not to think at all, as we lay there on the sand dunes at Sylt. . . . Later, he had to go East, and I was expecting our first child. On Christmas he came home on his last furlough—Christmas, 1942. In our entire marriage, how long were we together? Three months, perhaps, all told. We said good-bye at the railroad station—and just at that moment the sirens blared out—an air raid—but we paid no attention—we just stood there in the open. "Are you crazy?" I said to him. Martin was with us then —just a baby—the sky was full of flak, bombs were falling —there were direct hits on the bunkers—a whole chain of them, not two hundred yards from where we stood. "Too bad!" he said. I'll never forget that night. "But it's nothing," he said, and he gave me his hand—and a smile —like a man going to the gallows. . . . He was already through the gates before I knew he was gone—all I could do was scream his name. "Good luck!" he called. . . . Two months later, I got his last letter, from Warsaw—— [*She puts out her cigarette in an ash tray.*] Why do we keep telling these stories over and over? [STEPAN *sits on the arm of her chair.*]

STEPAN. War—not good.

AGNES. No.

STEPAN. Dirty war. [AGNES *takes his hand.*]

AGNES. Tell me about you. I will watch your mouth and understand everything you say. Jehuda says you're an engineer. And that you fought with the partisans. In the Crimea.

STEPAN. Crimea? [*He starts to sing a Crimean song, then breaks off abruptly.*] Mayà ròdina. [My homeland.]

AGNES. Tell me who you are. Where you come from. Tell me all about your life.

STEPAN. Crimea—kaput.

STEPAN *has risen and started to move about. Now he stops, arrested—a memory begins to come back to him. He starts*

to tell it, urged on by AGNES'*s questioning interest, adding
more and more by way of pantomime.*

STEPAN. Ya vyòl Partizànof. Vsorvàts most. Vdrùg nyemèt-
skiye tanki. Mi bezhàts chèriz lyòt. Lyòt nye dèrzhit. U
nàs dinamìt. Vadà vsyò vìshe: vot, vot . . . Water . . .
river . . . Syèm tavàrishchey gdyè? Na drugòm byeregù:
ya adìn. Adìn. Tavàrishchi? Tavàrishchi? Nyet. Tòlka vadà,
vadà i lyòt . . . [*He sits.*] vadà i lyòt—— [I led Partisans.
To blow up a bridge. Suddenly, German tanks. We run
across the ice. The ice doesn't hold. We have dynamite.
The water gets higher and higher: like this, like this . . .
Water . . . river. . . . Seven comrades, where? On the
other shore: I'm alone. Alone. Comrades? Comrades? No.
Only water, water and ice . . . water and ice.] Vadà i
lyòt. [*A knock. They listen. A knock again.*] Jehuda? [*A
third knock.*]

AGNES. Come in?

The door opens, and HORST *appears, wearing a gray business
suit.*

HORST. I beg your pardon . . . [*Pause.*] Colonel Ivanov?
[*Pause.*] After everything that I have heard about you . . .
my name is Anders. I suppose . . . [*Pause.*] Well, I was
wondering about the house, actually. If I may be so bold,
Colonel—I mean it of course merely as a question—well,
perhaps you yourself don't really know when the house
will be empty again. . . .

STEPAN *goes to the door.*

STEPAN. Jehuda! . . . Jehuda? [*He goes on out.*]

AGNES. What is this?

HORST. But I thought . . .

AGNES. Where did you get this suit?

HORST. You said he understood German.

STEPAN *returns angrily with* JEHUDA.

STEPAN. Chuzhòy chelavyèk. Chelavyèk sùlitsi vkhòdit
vnàshu kòmnatu. [A strange man. A man from off the
street has come into our room.]

JEHUDA. No vyet vsadù pastỳ. [But there are sentries in the
garden.]

STEPAN. Byez glàs. [Without eyes.]

JEHUDA. Nyepanyàtna. [Incomprehensible.]

STEPAN. Da. [Yes.]

JEHUDA *turns to* HORST.

JEHUDA. Comrade Commander will ask, who are you and what are you wishing?

HORST. I beg your pardon?

JEHUDA. Who are you and how have you come within this house?

HORST. That's what I'm telling you. My name is Anders. I am the master of this house. With your permission. I am this woman's husband.

JEHUDA. Anders?

HORST. Yes.

JEHUDA. Horst Anders?

HORST. Yes.

JEHUDA. Captain?

HORST. Yes. Why?

JEHUDA. Captain Anders—and you were in Warsaw? [JEHUDA *stares at him. His face becomes twisted into a grimace of hatred and fear. He takes the notebook from his pocket, crosses to the Colonel, and shows it to him.*] Girmànski afitsyèer. On bìl v Varshàvye. Ubìtsa. [A German officer. He was in Warsaw. A murderer.]

STEPAN. Atkùda znàyesh? [How do you know?]

JEHUDA. On yeyò mùzh! [He is her husband!]

JEHUDA *points to* AGNES. STEPAN *stands as though stunned by a blow.* JEHUDA *turns back to* HORST.

JEHUDA. Comrade Commander will know, is this true?

HORST. What?

JEHUDA. You were in Warsaw?

HORST. Yes——

JEHUDA. In March, nineteen and forty-three?

HORST. Why?

JEHUDA. You were in the ghetto? [HORST *hesitates.*] With the little pistols: ta ta ta. When we came out of the burning houses, eh: ta ta ta.

HORST. Not me—no!

JEHUDA. You knew?

HORST. Not me!

JEHUDA. Spring, nineteen and forty-three. March and April. Eighty thousand peoples . . .

AGNES. What does this mean, Horst? I don't understand this.

JEHUDA. Stroop Brigade.

HORST. But not the army troops!

JEHUDA. The army?

HORST. Yes—naturally, I was in the army. I can prove it! My uniform is down in the cellar. Go look!

JEHUDA. Yes—the army troops were there, too! I know—I was in the ghetto then. Rembertov Engineer Brigade. Right? Flak battery three-eight. Roman numeral three, Arabic numeral eight. Major Sternagel. Army, yes—Wehrmacht . . .

HORST. But not me! That's not true! I was in the hospital then, in the hospital in Warsaw, yes, with a wound in my arm——

JEHUDA. Can you prove this?

HORST. What——?

JEHUDA seizes him by the throat.

JEHUDA. You are murderer!

HORST draws the gun he has taken from AGNES.

HORST. Let me go. [*They all shrink back from him.*] What do you want from me?

AGNES suddenly steps in front of STEPAN.

AGNES. Horst!

HORST lets the pistol drop.

HORST. I am at your disposal——

A long silence. STEPAN turns to the window, his back to the room. AGNES looks across at him anxiously.

STEPAN. Mi ukhòdim. [*We're leaving.*]

JEHUDA, obeying with an effort at self-control, goes out through the sliding doors. STEPAN turns around slowly, his face drained of expression.

AGNES. Stepan Ivanov . . . ?

He slowly takes his cap, puts it on; takes his belt, snaps it on. All this without looking at either HORST or AGNES. Then he puts on his coat, crosses the room, and goes out.

HORST. Where is he going? [*AGNES is silent.*] You mean, he's going to leave us in peace? [*No answer.*] He's up to something—you watch——

JEHUDA *comes back, carrying the luggage; he crosses the room as though it were empty. He picks up the gun from the floor.*

AGNES. Jehuda . . . ?

He goes on out.

They are left alone, standing motionless, gazing at each other as though across an unbridgeable abyss.

Long silence.

Curtain.

DRAMABOOKS
(Plays)

When ordering, please use the Standard Book Number consisting of the publisher's prefix, 8090-, plus the five digits following each title. (Note that the numbers given in this list are for paperback editions only. Many of the books are also available in cloth.)

Mermaid Dramabooks

Christopher Marlowe (Tamburlaine the Great, Parts I & II, Doctor Faustus, The Jew of Malta, Edward the Second) (0701-0)

William Congreve (Complete Plays) (0702-9)

Webster and Tourneur (The White Devil, The Duchess of Malfi, The Atheist's Tragedy, The Revenger's Tragedy) (0703-7)

John Ford (The Lover's Melancholy, 'Tis Pity She's a Whore, The Broken Heart, Love's Sacrifice, Perkin Warbeck) (0704-5)

Richard Brinsley Sheridan (The Rivals, St. Patrick's Day, The Duenna, A Trip to Scarborough, The School for Scandal, The Critic) (0705-3)

Camille and Other Plays (Scribe: A Peculiar Position, The Glass of Water; Sardou: A Scrap of Paper; Dumas: Camille; Augier: Olympe's Marriage) (0706-1)

John Dryden (The Conquest of Granada, Parts I & II, Marriage à la Mode, Aureng-Zebe) (0707-X)

Ben Jonson Vol. 1 (Volpone, Epicoene, The Alchemist) (0708-8)

Oliver Goldsmith (The Good Natur'd Man, She Stoops to Conquer, An Essay on the Theatre, A Register of Scotch Marriages) (0709-6)

Jean Anouilh Vol. 1 (Antigone, Eurydice, The Rehearsal, Romeo and Jeannette, The Ermine) (0710-X)

Let's Get a Divorce! and Other Plays (Labiche: A Trip Abroad, and Célimare; Sardou: Let's Get a Divorce!; Courteline: These Cornfields; Feydeau: Keep an Eye on Amélie; Prévert: A United Family; Achard: Essays on Feydeau) (0711-8)

Jean Giraudoux Vol. 1 (Ondine, The Enchanted, The Madwoman of Chaillot, The Apollo of Bellac) (0712-6)

Jean Anouilh Vol. 2 (Restless Heart, Time Remembered, Ardèle, Mademoiselle Colombe, The Lark) (0713-4)

Henrik Ibsen: The Last Plays (Little Eyolf, John Gabriel Borkman, When We Dead Awaken) (0714-2)

Ivan Turgenev (A Month in the Country, A Provincial Lady, A Poor Gentleman) (0715-0)

Jean Racine (Andromache, Britannicus, Berenice, Phaedra, Athaliah) (0717-7)

The Storm and Other Russian Plays (The Storm, The Government Inspector, The Power of Darkness, Uncle Vanya, The Lower Depths) (0718-5)

Michel de Ghelderode: Seven Plays Vol. 1 (The Ostend Interviews, Chronicles of Hell, Barabbas, The Women at the Tomb, Pantagleize, The Blind Men, Three Players and a Play, Lord Halewyn) (0719-3)

Lope de Vega: Five Plays (Peribáñez, Fuenteovejuna, The Dog in the Manger, The Knight from Olmedo, Justice Without Revenge) (0720-7)

Calderón: Four Plays (Secret Vengeance for Secret Insult, Devotion to the Cross, The Mayor of Zalamea, The Phantom Lady) (0721-5)

Jean Cocteau: Five Plays (Orphée, Antigone, Intimate Relations, The Holy Terrors, The Eagle with Two Heads) (0722-3)

Ben Jonson Vol. 2 (Every Man in His Humour, Sejanus, Bartholomew Fair) (0723-1)

Port-Royal and Other Plays (Claudel: Tobias and Sara; Mauriac: Asmodée; Copeau: The Poor Little Man; Montherlant: Port-Royal) (0724-X)

Edwardian Plays (Maugham: Loaves and Fishes; Hankin: The Return of the Prodigal; Shaw: Getting Married; Pinero: Mid-Channel; Granville-Barker: The Madras House) (0725-8)

Georg Büchner: Complete Plays and Prose (0727-4)

Paul Green: Five Plays (Johnny Johnson, In Abraham's Bosom, Hymn to the Rising Sun, The House of Connelly, White Dresses) (0728-2)

François Billetdoux: Two Plays (Tchin-Tchin, Chez Torpe) (0729-0)

Michel de Ghelderode: Seven Plays Vol. 2 (Red Magic, Hop, Signor!, The Death of Doctor Faust, Christopher Columbus, A Night of Pity, Piet Bouteille, Miss Jairus) (0730-4)

Jean Giraudoux Vol. 2 (Siegfried, Amphitryon 38, Electra) (0731-2)

Kelly's Eye and Other Plays by Henry Livings (Kelly's Eye, Big Soft Nellie, There's No Room for You Here for a Start) (0732-0)

Gabriel Marcel: Three Plays (Man of God, Ariadne, Votive Candle) (0733-9)

New American Plays Vol. 1 ed. by Robert W. Corrigan (0734-7)

Elmer Rice: Three Plays (Adding Machine, Street Scene, Dream Girl) (0735-5)
The Day the Whores Came Out to Play Tennis . . . by Arthur Kopit (0736-3)
Platonov by Anton Chekhov (0737-1)
Ugo Betti: Three Plays (The Inquiry, Goat Island, The Gambler) (0738-X)
Jean Anouilh Vol. 3 (Thieves' Carnival, Medea, Cécile, Traveler Without Luggage, Orchestra, Episode in the Life of an Author, Catch As Catch Can) (0739-8)
Max Frisch: Three Plays (Don Juan, The Great Rage of Philip Hotz, When the War Was Over) (0740-1)
New American Plays Vol. 2 ed. by William M. Hoffman (0741-X)
Plays from Black Africa ed. by Fredric M. Litto (0742-8)
Anton Chekhov: Four Plays (The Seagull, Uncle Vanya, The Cherry Orchard, The Three Sisters) (0743-6)
The Silver Foxes Are Dead and Other Plays by Jakov Lind (The Silver Foxes Are Dead, Anna Laub, Hunger, Fear) (0744-4)
New American Plays Vol. 3 ed. by William M. Hoffman (0745-2)
The Modern Spanish Stage: Four Plays, ed. by Marion Holt (The Concert at Saint Ovide, Condemned Squad, The Blindfold, The Boat Without a Fisherman) (0746-0)
Life Is a Dream by Calderón (0747-9)
New American Plays Vol. 4 ed. by William M. Hoffman (0748-7)

THE NEW MERMAIDS
Bussy D'Ambois by George Chapman (1101-8)
The Broken Heart by John Ford (1102-6)
The Duchess of Malfi by John Webster (1103-4)
Doctor Faustus by Christopher Marlowe (1104-2)
The Alchemist by Ben Jonson (1105-0)
The Jew of Malta by Christopher Marlowe (1106-9)
The Revenger's Tragedy by Cyril Tourneur (1107-7)
A Game at Chess by Thomas Middleton (1108-5)
Every Man in His Humour by Ben Jonson (1109-3)
The White Devil by John Webster (1110-7)
Edward the Second by Christopher Marlowe (1111-5)
The Malcontent by John Marston (1112-3)
'Tis Pity She's a Whore by John Ford (1113-1)
Sejanus His Fall by Ben Jonson (1114-X)
Volpone by Ben Jonson (1115-8)
Women Beware Women by Thomas Middleton (1116-6)
Love for Love by William Congreve (1117-4)
The Spanish Tragedy by Thomas Kyd (1118-2)

SPOTLIGHT DRAMABOOKS
The Last Days of Lincoln by Mark Van Doren (1201-4)
Oh Dad, Poor Dad . . . by Arthur Kopit (1202-2)
The Chinese Wall by Max Frisch (1203-0)
Billy Budd by Louis O. Coxe and Robert Chapman (1204-9)
The Firebugs by Max Frisch (1205-6)
Andorra by Max Frisch (1207-3)
Balm in Gilead and Other Plays by Lanford Wilson (1208-1)
Matty and the Moron and Madonna by Herbert Lieberman (1209-X)
The Brig by Kenneth H. Brown (1210-3)
The Cavern by Jean Anouilh (1211-1)
Saved by Edward Bond (1212-X)
Eh? by Henry Livings (1213-8)
The Rimers of Eldritch and Other Plays by Lanford Wilson (1214-6)
In the Matter of J. Robert Oppenheimer by Heinar Kipphardt (1215-4)
Ergo by Jakov Lind (1216-2)
Biography: A Game by Max Frisch (1217-0)
Indians by Arthur Kopit (1218-9)
Narrow Road to the Deep North by Edward Bond (1219-7)
Ornifle by Jean Anouilh (1220-0)
Inquest by Donald Freed (1221-9)
Lemon Sky by Lanford Wilson (1222-7)
The Night Thoreau Spent in Jail by Jerome Laurence and Robert E. Lee (1223-5)

For a complete list of books of criticism and history of the drama, please write to Hill and Wang, 72 Fifth Avenue, New York, New York 10011.

6274- 075   53432